Special Events

Proven Strategies for Nonprofit Fund Raising

Wiley Nonprofit Law, Finance, and Management Series

The Art of Planned Giving: Understanding Donors and the Culture of Giving by Douglas E. White

Beyond Fund Raising: New Strategies for Nonprofit Investment and Innovation by Kay Grace

Charity, Advocacy, and the Law by Bruce R. Hopkins

The *Complete Guide to Fund Raising Management* by Stanley Weinstein

The Complete Guide to Nonprofit Management by Smith, Bucklin & Associates

Critical Issues in Fund Raising edited by Dwight Burlingame

Developing Affordable Housing: A Practical Guide for Nonprofit Organizations, Second Edition by Bennett L. Hecht

Financial and Accounting Guide for Not-for-Profit Organizations, Fifth Edition by Malvern J. Gross, Jr., Richard F. Larkin, Roger S. Bruttomesso, John J. McNally, Price Waterhouse L.L.P.

Financial Empowerment: More Money for More Mission by Peter C. Brinckerhoff

Financial Management for Nonprofit Organizations by Jo Ann Hankin, Alan Seidner, and John Zietlow

Financial Planning for Nonprofit Organizations by Jody Blazek

The Fund Raiser's Guide to the Internet by Michael Johnston

Fund-Raising: Evaluating and Managing the Fund Development Process by James M. Greenfield

Fund-Raising Fundamentals: A Guide to Annual Giving for Professionals and Volunteers by James M. Greenfield

Fund-Raising Regulation: A State-by-State Handbook of Registration Forms, Requirements, and Procedures by Seth Perlman and Betsy Hills Bush

Grantseeker's Toolkit: A Comprehensive Guide to Finding Funding by Cheryl S. New and James Quick

High Performance Nonprofit Organizations: Managing Upstream for Greater Impact by Christine Letts, Allen Grossman, and William Ryan

Intermediate Sanctions: Curbing Nonprofit Abuse by Bruce R. Hopkins and D. Benson Tesdahl

International Guide to Nonprofit Law by Lester A. Salamon and Stefan Toepler & Associates

The Law of Fund-Raising, Second Edition by Bruce R. Hopkins

The Law of Tax-Exempt Healthcare Organizations by Thomas K. Hyatt and Bruce R. Hopkins

Special Events

Proven Strategies for Nonprofit Fund Raising

Alan L. Wendroff

John Wiley & Sons, Inc.
New York • Chichester • Weinheim • Brisbane • Singapore • Toronto

Copyright © 1999 by John Wiley & Sons, Inc. All rights reserved.

Published simultaneously in Canada.

This publication is designed to provide accurate and authoritative information in regard to the subject matter covered. It is sold with the understanding that the publisher is not engaged in rendering professional services. If professional advice or other expert assistance is required, the services of a competent professional person should be sought.

Library of Congress Cataloging-in-Publication Data:

Wendroff, Alan L.
Special events : proven strategies for nonprofit fund raising /
Alan L. Wendroff.
    p. cm.—(Wiley nonprofit law, finance, and management
series)
  Includes bibliographical references (p.) and index.
  ISBN 0-471-24991-2
  1. Fund raising—United States. 2. Promotion of special events—
United States. 3. Nonprofit organizations—United States—Finance.
I. Title. II. Series: Nonprofit law, finance, and management series.
HV41.9.U5W47 1999
658.15'224—dc21   98-40651
                                                  CIP

Printed in the United States of America.

10 9 8 7 6 5 4 3 2 1

About the Author

Alan L. Wendroff, CFRE

Alan Wendroff is a people person who put on his first special event when he was a teenager in San Francisco. Over the years, he graduated to unpaid staff status with nonprofits and political campaigns.

He became a professional fundraiser in 1980, and in 1984 he became the area director of development for the Anti-Defamation League covering ten states and seventeen communities. In 1994 he hung out his shingle as an independent consultant for nonprofit agencies. Since then he has given workshops and lectured at the Support Center for Nonprofit Management, The Foundation Center, and the University of San Francisco's Institute of Nonprofit Organization Management–Development Directors Certificate program and the Masters program.

He serves on the board of directors of the Golden Gate Chapter of the National Society of Fund Raising Executives, a board member of the Central Pacific region of the Anti-Defamation League, and is a member of the United Way's Agency Relations Committee.

His consulting clients are diverse, ranging from arts and professional organizations to human relations and health agencies.

Alan and his wife Lyllian live on a hilltop in his native city of San Francisco.

Dedication

To Lyllian Wendroff, my partner in life whose love and belief in my abilities gave me the inspiration to start and complete this book. All my love!

Contents

Preface

This is a book for people involved with nonprofit agencies: The lay leadership and professional staff people who are the backbone of philanthropy around the world. They strive to achieve success with their fund raising programs, especially the special events they have been producing or want to put on for the first time. In fund raising the typical fund raiser thinks that success is raising more money with the current fund raising event than they did with the last one. This is only one-seventh true; there are at least six other goals that make special event fund raising a success: An up-to-date, easily understandable, Mission Statement, motivation of the lay leadership and professionals, recruitment of more volunteers, expanding the nonprofit's network of supporters, marketing the agency to the community, and endorsements by VIPs and community and business leaders. Together, these seven goals are the heart of the nonprofit's strategic fund-raising plan.

The foundation of successful fund raising is face to face solicitation. It is the first lesson beginning fund raisers learn, along with the technique, that talking to a current or potential contributor, is a lay leaders responsibility along with the assistance of an agency professional: Either the executive director or fund raiser. It is a team effort. There is no substitute for the solicitor looking into the eye's of a donor and telling that person why he or she supports the nonprofit; and, why the potential donor should join the solicitor in the financial support of the agency. Nonprofit's, even the very largest agencies, do not have enough staff or trained volunteers to accomplish a face to face solicitation with every contributor, past, present, or potential. Special events can raise the ratio of personal contacts from its current low status to one where at least the nonprofit can tell its story and relate its mission to a much larger audience of interested donors.

Special events are the *only* fund raising program where potential givers come to your "place," pay for the privilege of listening and learning what your agency is accomplishing. Do not let this opportunity disappear for lack of planning.

This book gives the agency and its supporters and professional staff tools that will enable them to plan their event to achieve the seven goals. This is the basis for potential stewardship of the guests that attend the special event.

This book is organized so that the reader can begin with the introduction and go through each chapter and build their special event in a logical way from start to finish; although, a special event is never finished in the sense that if it is used to its best advantage, it will continue to link volunteer and supporter to the nonprofit for many years.

The special resource section contains documents that can be used with almost every chapter of the book, and can be used with the agency's current on-going event as a reality check.

There are millions of people volunteering and giving to nonprofit agencies each year throughout the United States. Why doesn't your agency grow in these areas each year? Why aren't volunteers knocking down your door? Why is the number of gifts your agency receives each year stagnated at a plateau and never increases? Two reasons: The agency hasn't developed a clear, concise, and doable fund-raising plan, and secondly, the people you want to volunteer and contribute haven't been asked, because there is no clear, concise, and doable fund-raising plan.

Avoid going around in circles and getting nowhere! Make the special event the centerpiece of your development plan, and build the other fund raising programs to feed off the networking and recruitment results of the event. The components of an annual fund raising plan include: Face to face solicitations for major and capital gifts, planned giving, direct mail, and telephone solicitations. Build up a prospect list from the names received from the event chair(s) and committee members. The latest figures on giving and volunteering indicate that nearly seven out of ten households in the United States (68.2 million) reported contributions in 1995. (Source: Independent Sector: Giving and Volunteering in the United States, 1996.) The nonprofit that makes itself known through the marketing of its community programs (and its fund raising events) will be in a position to tap into this enormous number of potential supporters and volunteers.

Once goal oriented planning is a part of your organization's strategy good things will begin to occur, because the agency planned them to happen.

Alan L. Wendroff
San Francisco, California

Acknowledgments

This book could not have been written without the advice, help, and inspiration of many friends and colleagues. They were kind enough to read parts of the text, comment on it, make suggestions, and clarify many points of professional practice. Thank you, one and all, for your valuable time.

Usually, a writer will acknowledge their editor after they have thanked everyone else; I could not have gotten to this point in this book without the guidance, patience, understanding, encouragement, and long distance hand holding I received from my editor, Martha Cooley. Martha redirected the flow of the book from a stuttering unsure collection of pages to the smooth logical presentation it has become. Thank you, Martha!

Thank you, Hank Rosso for giving so generously of your valuable time reading the basic tenets on which this book is based, your advice and suggestions have been a reality check which I have treasured and followed.

Thank you, Kay Grace Beaumont for having believed in this project from the minute you read the outline and did me the kindness of introducing me to my editor and publisher.

Thank you, Gwyneth J. Lister and Eliot M. "Skip" Henderson for inviting me to talk to your fund raising classes at the University of San Francisco, where many of the ideas contained in this book were explained and put to the test of student criticism. The result has been a clearer exposition of some technical ideas and concepts, such as estimating attendance and the budget process.

Thank you, Michael D. Dellar for letting me use your from the heart thank you letter.

Thank you, Joanne Handy, Judy Loura, Jim Hilferty, Denize Springer, and those wonderful Dinner à la Heart volunteers, Sandra Simon and Roean Iscoff, at the Goldman Institute on Aging, San Francisco.

Thank you, Laurence Whiting and Tom Brooker of Now We're Cooking!, San Francisco's premier catering company, for your creative graphics, sample documents, and helpful advice on catering matters.

Thank you, Douglas E. Goldman, M.D., and Theodore G. Arbuckle of Certain Software™, Inc., publishers of Event Planner Plus™ for letting me reproduce the ballroom set-up illustration from that program.

Thank you, Michael Romo of the St. Vincent de Paul Society, San Francisco, for letting me reproduce various documents from the Frank Brennan award dinner.

Thank you, to all of my friends and colleagues at the Anti-Defamation League for giving permission to reproduce some of their creative special event invitations.

Thank you, Sue Petersen, Executive Director of the San Francisco Giants Community Fund, and GE Capital, for the reproduction of the 1998 Giants Community Fund Golf Classic invitation.

Thank you, to my friends who took the time to advise, read, and comment on various sections of the manuscript: Fran Abenheimer, James Scott Armstrong, CFRE, Ron Berman, Ken Deutsch, Dan De Vries, Terri Forman, CFRE, Ellen Hertzman, Gwen Kaplan, Edwin Kiester, Jr., Joseph R. Mixer, Howard N. Nemerovski, Susan Kalmus Partier, Norman Schlossberg, Midge Stone, Debbi Waldbaum, Samuel R. T. Singer, David P. Wendroff, and Michael A. Zimmerman.

Special Events

Proven Strategies for Nonprofit Fund Raising

INTRODUCTION

Special Event Fund Raising—A Beginning

"It is a fund raiser enveloped in a dinner inside of seven goals."
—with apologies to Sir Winston Churchill

A FEW DEFINITIONS FOR FUND RAISING SPECIAL EVENTS

A nonprofit special event is a unique fund-raising program that strengthens the nonprofit's image in the community and recruits and involves volunteers[1]; it raises money as well as friends.[2] Special events involve bringing together lay leaders, volunteers, and the nonprofit's supporters in a social gathering that entertains and educates people regarding the work of the nonprofit in the community. Special event fund raising is centered around the organization of volunteer lay leadership, the people who populate a nonprofit agency's board of directors or committees or who just lend a helping hand because they believe in the mission of the organization. In this way, a special event brings to life the nonprofit's mission.

Special events can be presented as tribute and award programs (breakfasts, lunches, dinners, or receptions), an annual board meeting, a tennis or golf tournament, a 10K run or walk, an auction, or a combination of all of these models, which "challenges the creative energies of enthusiastic volunteers" and "bind[s] them closer to the organization."[3]

The goal of most special events is to raise money; however, raising money does not necessarily have to be an "in-your-face" activity. It can introduce the prospective donor to the concept of stewardship or raising friends. Special events, if planned creatively, will explain the work of the nonprofit in a setting that is informative, relaxed, and often fun with the result being that funds are raised. This is creative marketing!

Special events should be part of a nonprofit's overall development program. The same principles that govern the design and organization of special events can apply to other nonprofit fund-raising and non–fund-raising programs: major and capital gifts solicitations, the board's annual meeting, and the annual fund-raising campaign, which includes direct mail, telethons, and one-on-one solicitations.

SEVEN GOALS FOR A SUCCESSFUL SPECIAL EVENT

1. Raise Money
2. Update the Mission Statement to Educate Your Constituency
3. Motivate Board Members and Major Givers
4. Recruit Volunteers and Future Board Members
5. Expand the Organization's Network
6. Market the Organization
7. Solicit Endorsements

Board and professional staff members of nonprofit organizations often wonder whether the time and effort spent on a special event is worth it. When handled properly, special events can achieve the monetary goal, plus much more, which is why these events are called *special*. The special character of fund-raising events is that multidimensional goals can result from designing and implementing a strategy that affects all of the guests who attend the event. Board members often remark that they only see or hear from supporters at the annual special event, and say that while it is nice to cash their checks and fund the agency's budget, why not just telephone these people and ask them to mail in the cost of the reservation and be done with it? Realistically, however, only a small percentage of people telephoned will mail a check, and those who do probably will send less than the net amount the agency receives from producing the event. The most important point—and one that many nonprofit boards often overlook—is the personal contact that a special event can offer, in contrast, to the usual arm's-length direct mail or telethon programs.

The need for personal contact with the organization lies with the herd instinct of people: They like and want to get together and socialize, especially if the socializing means that they can hobnob with prominent community and industry leaders and celebrities. And if they also can support a nonprofit that is doing good in their community, all the better! Once the guests are there, what should the nonprofit do with them?

Making supporters out of guests is the ultimate aim of the seven goals. The goals define the reason why a nonprofit should put on a special event; how to put on a special event is described in detail in the following chapters of this book. The Seven Goals are the foundation of special event fund raising practice, the Key Elements found in Chapter 2 are the administrative duties that build on the foundation, and the Master Event Timetable is the blueprint that should be followed to achieve the desired results. The seven goals include:

1. **Raise funds now, and raise more funds later.** Raising funds is a very straightforward, legitimate goal for any nonprofit fund-raising special event program. Special events change the method of obtaining gifts because raising money is just one of seven goals in the special event matrix; the events also alter the way prospective donors interact with the agency's entire development program.

Special event fund raising takes the form of an "entrance fee"; it is a hybrid, part nondeductible fee for a tangible item (food, auction bids, green fees) and part pure gift to the nonprofit. It assumes that a minimum number of paying guests will attend the event and reduce the per-person cost of set overhead costs—that is, site rental, decorations, and photography. If these costs amount to $1,000, and 100 guests attend the event, the fixed overhead amounts to $10 per person. However, if 350 guests attend, then the overhead is only $2.86 per person! Quite a reduction. The fixed costs of meals do not change; they are set relative to the anticipated number of guests. Referring to the example, if 100 guests attend, the meal costs $45, plus $10 for overhead costs, for a total of $55. If 350 guests attend, the total costs are only $47.86. If the per-seat charge for the event is $100, the net return to the agency increases with every seat sold. (See Chapter 3 for a detailed discussion of budgets.)

Special event fund raising is a major element of an organization's development plan, which includes: capital and major gift campaigns, planned giving, and endowments, all of which target intended donors after a relatively long period of stewardship. Annual and direct mail campaigns are immediate solutions to raising funds for the nonprofit. Many people prefer to give in an "arm's-length," semiautonomous manner, and respond more favorably to a telephone conversation or a personal letter from a friend or acquaintance. Thus, getting these people to attend a special event is a twofold stewardship process. After these once-a-year supporters are convinced to attend a special event, they may become more receptive to a continuing stewardship process: giving and participating.

For the new prospect or the donor who gives but knows very little about the agency, attending an event for the first time is the beginning of the stewardship process, because the event is often the first personal introduction this donor has to the nonprofit and its mission. Special event fund raising is the first step along the path that, with honest stewardship, can lead to future major and capital gifts and planned giving.

The individual donor or the corporate contributor has a choice as to whether to come to the event or not. Getting donors to attend is like getting them to read past the first paragraph of a direct mail solicitation.

2. Educate the public about the nonprofit's mission. This goal takes the special event fund-raising process to a higher level. It becomes a forum where the mission statement is interpreted and translated from words in the nonprofit's annual report to concrete examples of the organization's work in the community.

It is valuable to have an interface at the event between the guests and the nonprofit. During a reception period preceding the main event, dinner, golf tournament, auction, or theater party, a table or booth can be set up, staffed by senior professionals and lay leaders. The table or booth should have an attraction—such as photographs, a video or film playing, or a poster—to alert the guests that there is something going on besides small talk. This interface area should be well supplied with copies of the mission statement (and case statements if the agency is planning a future capital campaign or any special fund-raising campaign), current newsletters, an in-house folder of newspaper clippings, and brochures usually mailed to potential supporters.

The other essential education element takes the form of an eight- to ten-minute talk at the event about the work of the agency, given by the executive director and/or a well-informed lay leader (the president of the board, for example). Be rigid about the time—only eight to ten minutes; guests' attention span at special events is very limited. After this presentation, the lay leader at each table can engage the guests in conversation about the speaker's subject.

3.   **Motivate board members and major givers.** One of the requirements of board membership is fund raising! A frequent objection that anguished executives and development directors hear is: "I just can't ask my friends or, for that matter, strangers for money." Special events are friendly, not intimidating. Selling tickets to special events is an excellent way to train shy and reluctant board members and volunteers in the art of fund raising.

When an in-house annual campaign is planned, these reluctant people are protected by a group they know and the cries become louder. However, when these same complainers become a part of a special event committee, made up of members from major corporations and other prominent citizens, they are less likely to complain. Instead, they are caught up in the activity of a committee meeting populated by their peers who have no qualms about asking people for money to support a special event for "their" nonprofit. And when solicitors receive positive feedback and sell their first ticket, they are encouraged to ask for more when making the next telephone call.

4.   **Recruit volunteers and future board members.** Volunteers are the fuel that drives the engine of all nonprofit programs; recruitments can serve to expand the quantity and quality of the pool of volunteers. One reason to have a well-informed lay leader sit at every table or be part of every golf foursome is to identify the guests who suddenly discover the agency and its good work, and who want to become a part of this program this very minute. Who is the best person to guide these recent converts to the volunteer pool? The experienced lay leader, who is part of their immediate group at the special event and can engage them in conversation at a formal event in an informal, relaxed setting. Remember, volunteers often become board members, and special events are an excellent milieu in which lay leaders can meet, talk, and recruit the next generation of leaders.

5.   **Expand the organization's network.** Build a donor base. To expand, nonprofits need names of potential donors. Special events are designed to bring together large groups of people. Chapter 4 explains the networking process that is an inherent factor for successful recruit-

ment of the event committee. These names can legitimately be added to an existing prospect list. Each committee member on an active committee will provide an average of six to nine new names (from the ten requested of them); this in itself is a good reason to recruit the largest possible committee. It is not unusual for one or two committee members to give many more names than the ten requested. Event chairs are an excellent source for names for the prospect list; in fact, it is one of their duties to provide the agency with their personal nonprofit invitation list.

6. **Market the organization.** Marketing is closely linked with the first goal, raising money, and the second goal, promoting the agency's mission statement. A special event is one of a nonprofit's primary marketing tools. It provides a natural venue to bring together prospects, current and past supporters, and people who are new to the special world of philanthropy. It allows these people to see firsthand the work of the agency, by letting them observe the agency, its lay leaders, and staff in a controlled situation where the agency is shown to its best advantage. For example, booths should be set up, where staff managers can explain their particular programs; agency literature should be provided for each table; and, most important, if possible, a board member or longtime supporter, someone who can articulate the agency's philosophy and mission, should be seated at each table. This is especially important if members of the press attend the event. The press should never sit together at a table, wander around with a still or video camera, or interview the honoree, guest speaker, or board president without a senior member of the agency's staff guiding them. A media kit should be prepared. (Chapter 6 explains how to do this.)

Public relations is the advertising side of the coin that teaches the public about the special event. A special event is either planned for the general public—that is, to draw as many participants as possible—or designed for a specific group, such as the agency's natural constituency, prospects, and current givers. In the first situation, it is optimal that every newspaper, television, and radio station support the event by promoting it. Ever wonder why "society" types always have their favorite nonprofit special event mentioned in the gossip columns? High society is news! Often, its members are prominent corporate citizens who advertise in the media. But how does the worthy but plain-vanilla nonprofit, without any society members on its board, get space or air time in the media? One way is to hire a public relations consultant firm to champion the cause; a better way is to recruit a PR person to join the board. Either way, the focus should be a program that best addresses the work the agency accomplishes in the entire community.

An organization's own constituents—those who currently support the agency and those who have been mailed appeals—are by far the easiest groups to reach with a public relations message regarding an upcoming special event. An in-house newsletter, networking by the board of directors, and the tried-and-true telephone tree can be the forerunners of the special event's own public relations materials.

7. **Make endorsements.** At honoree events—either tribute or award functions, or at tournaments, auctions, and theater parties where a prominent community citizen serves as the master of ceremonies, or where a celebrity is in attendance—there is no better way to achieve stature in the community than to have this celebrity, in addition to the honoree, stand up and proclaim his or her support for the work of the agency. An organization cannot buy such a recommendation. This is a public relations bonanza for the nonprofit: a prominent community citizen or celebrity receiving an award from the agency, especially when a photo appears in the local newspaper the next day or in the Sunday edition.

These Seven Goals are the heart of the special event fund raising program. Together they give meaning to this program that can produce so many future benefits for the nonprofit. To illustrate these benefits, the following example of a creative special event, *Dinner à la Heart,* will explain in detail the seven goals as they apply to an actual annual special event. Building a nonprofit's stature in the community does not happen overnight, it is a long term process, and to achieve community support the agency must take the first step, either by producing their first special event, or redesigning the one they have been putting on each year.

DINNER À LA HEART: A CREATIVE SPECIAL EVENT

Dinner à la Heart (see invitation in Exhibit A) is an excellent example of a creative special event because it illustrates the first six goals just outlined as the basic objectives and the backbone of a successful special event. Although there is no honoree in this example (goal 7), there could have been a celebrity chairperson, honorary, or otherwise, which would illustrate the seventh goal as described in the previous section.

Goal 1: Raise Money

Designing an event around what a community has—not reinventing the wheel—is what separates the struggling nonprofit from the successful one. Nonprofits often overlook this type of creativity, to their

Exhibit A   Invitation to Dinner à la Heart

YOU ARE CORDIALLY INVITED TO
THE 15TH ANNUAL

DINNER À LA HEART

TUESDAY, FEBRUARY 10, 1998
7 PM

KING & QUEEN OF HEARTS
Gwen & John Kerner, MD

SPONSORS
Bill & Fay Polse

PATRONS
Bank of America
Jurika & Voyles
   Investment Mgmt.
PG&E

BENEFACTORS
Richard C. Blum &
   Associates, L.P.
Andrea Harris
See's Candies
Sutro & Co.

FRIENDS
Judy & Harry Camp
Steven J. Cohen
Good & Fowler CPA's
Frances & William Green
Barbara & John Greenberg
Eve & Vernon Heyman
The Men's Wearhouse
Mr. & Mrs. Alan Silver
Daniel E. Stone
Wells Fargo Capital Mgmt.
William Shine Co.,
   Tax & Estate Planning

DINNER
À LA HEART

GOLDMAN INSTITUTE ON AGING ASSOCIATES

Thelma Colvin, Chair
Sandra Simon, Chair, Dinner à la Heart

Melanie Burk Adler ♥ Margery D. Anson ♥
Marion Baer ♥ Barbara Barron ♥ Doris Blum
♥ Leonard F. Creed ♥ Frances Green ♥
Barbara Greenberg ♥ Lorraine Guggenheim
♥ Eve Heyman ♥ Roean Iscoff ♥ Dorothy Krieger
♥ Suzanne Landson ♥ Jeane Lapkin ♥
Inge Lehmann ♥ Helene Messinger ♥
Bobie Nathan ♥ Jane Peiser ♥
Hinda Silberstein-Waite ♥ Audrey Sockolov
♥ Ethel Wallace ♥ Judy Williams

Exhibit A *(continued)*

THE GOLDMAN INSTITUTE ON AGING ASSOCIATES
invite you to create your own festive party
or intimate dinner.

OUR VISION AT THE GOLDMAN INSTITUTE
on Aging is to assure that aging be as
healthy and independent as possible.
To realize this mission, we create and
provide innovative programs in health,
social services, education and research.
These programs enable seniors to remain
in their homes and communities while
living life to the fullest.

YOUR DONATION TO DINNER À LA HEART
this year will support SeniorHealth,
the IOA's comprehensive program
that provides the full range of medical
services, as well as social and
recreational opportunities to seniors
in a day care setting.

$50 provides a wheelchair rental

$70 provides a shower chair for clients
treated at home

$90 provides one week's speech therapy
for two clients

$125 provides a pair of glasses for
two clients

DINNER
À LA HEART

Used with permission from Goldman Institute on Aging.

detriment. Organizations often think that glitzy, celebrity-driven events are the only ones supporters will attend. They plan and spend money to produce these extravaganzas, and when the event is over and the accounting is finished, not only do they realize they did not raise a significant amount of money, but they did not achieve any substantive objectives. On the Tuesday of St. Valentine's week, 900-plus supporters attended an event benefiting the Goldman Institute on Aging. This was the fifteenth annual year of this creative and unique event. Dinner à la Heart raised $75,000 net proceeds and involved 69 restaurants located in five counties around the San Francisco Bay Area. Dinner à la Heart draws on the community's strength. (In San Francisco, there are more than 4,000 restaurants.) The beauty of this event is obvious: People like to eat at popular, gourmet restaurants; many times during the year, they will treat themselves to a night out. What better way to do this than to have

Exhibit B   Dinner à la Heart Reservation Contributions

A limited number of seats are reserved at the following restaurants. Those marked with an * have ten or less seats available. Reservations are on a first-come, first-served basis beginning January 5, 1998. Priority will be given to contributors of $5,000 or more. For more information call: (415) 750-4117.

$50 PER PERSON

Bistro Alsacien
Cacti Restaurant (Novato)
Café de Paris"L'Entrecote"
Chateau Suzanne
Fly Trap
Frantoio (Mill Valley)
Garibaldi's on Presidio
Garibaldi's (Oakland)
Giorgios (San Mateo)
Helmand*
House of Prime Rib*
Il Fornaio (Burlingame)
Il Fornaio (San Francisco)
Joe LoCoco's (Greenbrae)
Le Central Bistro
Left Bank (Larkspur)
MacArthur Park
   Restaurant
Marina Central
The Meetinghouse*
Nathan's on the Avenue
   (Burlingame)
Oberon Restarant & Bar
Occidental Grill
Pane E Vino Trattoria*
Piatti Mill Valley
Radicchio Trattoria*
Rocco's Seafood Grill
Ton Kiang
Venticello Ristorante
Washington Square
   Bar & Grill
Zibibbo* (Palo Alto)

DINNER
À LA HEART

a great meal with friends *and* support a nonprofit at the same time? Exhibit B shows the depth and strength of restaurant choices that the Goldman Institute was able to capitalize on and the response card that highlighted the variety of choices.

Because Dinner à la Heart is different in many ways from the usual special event, an example of an actual budget from a recent year's event is shown in Exhibit C.

Revenue sources are dependent on the interaction between a restaurant's donations of free and discounted dinners and the guests who attend the event. In this case, what comes first, the chicken or the egg? is easy to answer: the egg! People will support an event like this if the choice of restaurants is superior; that is, the venues must have a reputation for serving gourmet food in an ambiance that is fun and pleasing for the guest. Dinner à la Heart solicits free dinners and

Exhibit B *(continued)*

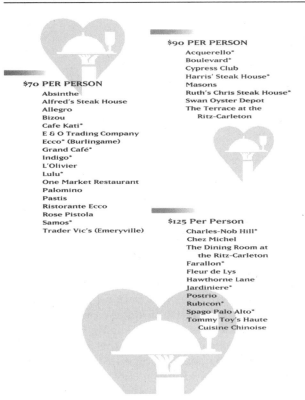

$90 PER PERSON
Acquerello*
Boulevard*
Cypress Club
Harris' Steak House*
Masons
Ruth's Chris Steak House*
Swan Oyster Depot
The Terrace at the
   Ritz-Carleton

$70 PER PERSON
Absinthe
Alfred's Steak House
Allegro
Bizou
Cafe Kati*
E & O Trading Company
Ecco* (Burlingame)
Grand Café*
Indigo*
L'Olivier
Lulu*
One Market Restaurant
Palomino
Pastis
Ristorante Ecco
Rose Pistola
Samos*
Trader Vic's (Emeryville)

$125 Per Person
Charles-Nob Hill*
Chez Michel
The Dining Room at
   the Ritz-Carleton
Farallon*
Fleur de Lys
Hawthorne Lane
Jardiniere*
Postrio
Rubicon*
Spago Palo Alto*
Tommy Toy's Haute
   Cuisine Chinoise

Exhibit B *(continued)*

DINNER À LA HEART
February 10, 1998

PLEASE RESERVE:

places at $50 ($25 is tax deductible)
places at $70 ($35 is tax deductible)
places at $90 ($45 is tax deductible)
places at $125 ($62.50 is tax deductible)

CHOICE OF RESTAURANT (in order of preference):

1. _____
2. _____
3. _____

____Check (payable to Goldman Institute on Aging Associates)
____Mastercard/Visa #_____ Exp. _____

Name_____

Address _____

City/State/Zip _____

Daytime phone _____

I am unable to attend, but a contribution of $_____ is enclosed.

Phone reservations (credit cards only) will be accepted starting on Monday, January 5, 1998. Please call 415/750-4117.

♥ No-Host Bar. Dinner includes one glass of wine, tax, and gratuity.
♥ Forming a party? Please provide guests' name, address and phone.
♥ If you are attending as a guest, a donation would be appreciated.
♥ Event underwriters of $5,000 or more will be given seating priority.

Used with permission from Goldman Institute on Aging.

accepts discounted donations that are given at half price for the complete entrée, including wine, dessert, and tip. Many restaurants donate a combination of no-cost and discounted dinners. The budget shows three revenue lines and an in-kind offset line. The in-kind amount is shown for reference purposes so that a complete financial picture is presented. Individual dinner reservations at 62 percent leads the revenues, followed by underwriting revenue from individuals and corporations that donate special gifts ranging from $500 to $10,000. These donors receive special benefits in the form of name recognition in various publications and, in some instances, guaranteed dinners at the restaurant of the donor's choice. The donation line is just that: donations sent from people who cannot attend the event.

Exhibit C   Dinner à la Heart: Revenue and Expense Budget Items

	A	B	C	D	E	F	G	H
1								
2								
3								
4	REVENUE SOURCES:					Percentage of Total Revenue		
5							⇓	
6	Individual Dinner Reservations:					$71,310.00	62.36%	
7								
8	Underwriting Revenue					$30,000.00	26.23%	
9								
10	Donations					$10,051.00	8.79%	
11								
12								
13								
14								
15			Total Revenue=			$111,361.00		
16	In-Kind:					$3,000.00	2.62%	
17								
18	TOTAL REVENUE:					$114,361.00	100.00%	
19								
20								
21	EXPENSES:					Percentage of expense divided by total revenue		
22							⇓	
23	Restaurants					$28,401.07	24.83%	
24								
25	Printing:							
26	Save the Date & other cards:					$58.05	0.05%	
27	Contracts & Menus					$744.77	0.65%	
28	Invitations					$1,230.94	1.08%	
29	Posters					$19.53	0.02%	
30	Table Tents					$235.12	0.21%	
31								
32	Advertising					$410.00		
33								
34	Mailing House including postage:							
35	Save-the-date mailing					$260.00	0.23%	
36	Invitations					$2,180.51	1.91%	
37	Decorations & Ambiance:							
38	Flowers					$248.57	0.22%	
39	Photographer					$579.39	0.51%	
40	Balloons					$732.56	0.64%	
41	Miscellaneous items:							
42	Refunds & reimbursements					$490.67	0.43%	
43					Sub-T	$35,591.18	31.12%	
44	In-Kind Offset:					$(3,000.00)		
45								
46	TOTAL EXPENSE:					$38,591.18	33.75%	
47								
48	NET REVENUE:					$75,769.82	66.25%	

Used with permission from Goldman Institute on Aging.

Expenses for this event were reasonable, slightly under 34 percent for an overall gross return of 66 percent of total revenue. If the in-kind donations are taken into account, the percentages rise about 3.5 percent for revenue, and expenses are reduced by the same amount. The net return on restaurant dinners is very good:

Cost of dinners: $28,401.00

Restaurant reservation income: $71,310.00

for a 39.8 percent cost factor; or put another way,
a 60.2 percent net revenue gain

Considering that Dinner à la Heart met six goals and has the capacity to achieve all seven goals, the event is a great success for the Goldman Institute on Aging.

Goal 2: Update the Mission Statement to Educate Your Constituency

Dinner à la Heart is an intimate event that allows the nonprofit to make its case on an almost one-on-one basis. Approximately 10 to 50 guests eat at a restaurant. Instead of listening to a speech, attendees can learn about the agency from one of its active supporters or professional staff members. Breaking bread with a knowledgeable dinner partner is a more natural way to have the nonprofit's mission statement brought to life. This event also appeals to people who are able to support the organization in the future with larger gifts because they are approached in a more sophisticated manner. Because attendees can talk face to face to a prospect, Dinner à la Heart is the first step in a stewardship process that will allow the agency to set up a major gift solicitation at a future date.

Goal 3: Motivate Board Members and Major Givers

In addition to the volunteers, board members and the agency's major supporters participate in hosting or selling tickets to this event. Volunteers are often regular customers at restaurants that support this event, and hence are good at recruiting their participation. (See Exhibit D.) The price to attend Dinner à la Heart is relatively low; in addition, the guest receives a tax deduction on that portion in excess of the actual cost of the dinner. Consequently, the volunteer solicitor receives more yes than no

Exhibit D   Dinner à la Heart: Restaurant Patronizing Card

As a supporter of the Goldman Institute on Aging, I had the pleasure of attending its annual February benefit, Dinner á la Heart. I very much appreciate that your restaurant was involved and plan to show my gratitude by patronizing and recommending your establishment whenever I have the opportunity.

Used with permission from Goldman Institute on Aging.

replies. Thus, the event becomes an excellent way to motivate these supporters to get involved in the more relevant major gift solicitation process.

Goal 4: Recruit Volunteers and Future Board Members

Recruitment of volunteers can and should take place at this event. In order to recruit effectively at Dinner à la Heart, the agency should make sure that a board member or senior volunteer is present at each restaurant, so that when guests exclaim how interested they are in the work of the nonprofit, the designated agency representative can talk to them and learn what their interests are and how much time they have available to volunteer, and can explain what the nonprofit can offer them. (Remember to get the person's vital statistics: name, address, and contact numbers—telephone, fax, cellular, pager, and e-mail.) This is a once-in-a-lifetime opportunity; do not let it slip by. A strategy must be in place to contact guests again. The dynamics of talking about an agency in a group setting often motivates people to join with their peers in accomplishing the good work the agency does in the community.

Goal 5: Expand the Organization's Network

One reason more than 900 people attend Dinner à la Heart is networking. When longtime supporters purchase tables or multiple seats, the names and addresses of the guests they bring end up on the Goldman

Institute's database. This year's guests become next year's table purchasers or, better yet, annual fund donors.

Goal 6: Market the Organization

Events like Dinner à la Heart are short on speeches and long on printed material and table talk. One of the reasons people come back year after year is that they have fun! Marketing an organization and having fun do not have to be mutually exclusive. Each table should have a current brochure that describes the agency; or a new one emphasizing a program that is unique and of general interest to the community can be designed. Icebreakers at each table are also helpful. This is another reason it is so important to have a board member or senior volunteer at each table: After the usual small talk, there is usually a pause when guests are searching for something else to talk about, so why not make sure it is the agency! At the last Dinner à la Heart the writer attended, guests were greeted by a volunteer who introduced herself and made sure we were seated at the correct table and that everything was in order.

WHO WILL BENEFIT FROM THIS BOOK

This book is written for nonprofit professionals and their support staffs, plus volunteer laypeople—in short, everyone who is involved with a nonprofit organization. Special events can help an organization produce more than funds if they are designed and implemented correctly. That is what the seven goals defined in this chapter are all about. It is a fact that a nonprofit can achieve greater net proceeds—that is, *bottom line monetary* results—for their current needs with other fund-raising programs such as face-to-face solicitations, direct mail, foundation support, and telethons. However, special events take nonprofit fund raising to a people-to-people level where, in a nonconfrontational atmosphere, the agency lays the groundwork for recruiting a solid, long-term supporter who will give of him- or herself in the form of association and time with the agency. Opening doors to people who have not previously been associated with the nonprofit, through attendance at a special event, places them on the same level as those who give substantial gifts to the organization. This can be the beginning of donor stewardship. The rewards can be greater still if the agency makes that extra effort to introduce decision makers, prospective supporters, and the community to a special event where they can meet the nonprofit's lay leadership, people like them who are volunteering their time, energy, and financial support. If the event is properly planned (one of the pillars of this book; see Chapter 2) they also will meet the agency's professional staff and learn firsthand of the agency's value to the community. When this special-event model of organization and planning is applied to the nonprofit's overall development plan, the organization will achieve all seven of the goals introduced in this book.

HOW TO USE THIS BOOK: AN OVERVIEW

The sequence of events, from this introduction through Chapters 1 to 10 establishes a proven strategy from the launch of an organization's special event to its conclusion. It is impossible to look over everyone's shoulder and make "do" or "never do that" comments, this book makes use of a device called the Master Event Timetable (METT). The METT will never shout at you, or berate your efforts; it will just be there as a permanent reminder that, for example, in week 1 for the event to be successful, such and such a task must be done!

Many tools created for this book are linked to the subject areas discussed in each chapter. Furthermore, the exhibits have been formatted in MS Excel '97 spreadsheets on the disk included with the book. The following is a summary of these tools.

METT Checklist for Introduction Section

Week 1	To Do This Week	Book Ref.	☑
a)	Governing board meets with, or appoints, development committee and establishes parameters for the type of special event to produce and the goals that need to be achieved to make the event a success. Review Seven Goals. Using generic METT as a guide, make sure that all preliminary ideas, potential list of volunteers, event site[s], and potential dates are available at this meeting, even if they are only tentative. If the nonprofit's Mission Statement needs updating, this is the meeting to suggest the new wording.	Intro.	

This introduction introduced the reader to special events as one of the primary programs in a nonprofit's development strategy. It also described the basic philosophy of this book: seven goals for special events. These goals explained the results that nonprofit governing committees must strive for when they are planning the overall development plan, and the special event in particular. It then examined a unique special event, one that uses what a community has to offer; for example: the inherent difference each locale used to its advantage. The METT was briefly introduced and will be explained in detail throughout. It is referred to in every chapter as a reference guide for the reader; some chapters have subsets of METT if more detailed tasks must be accomplished.

Chapter 1 explains how to use the METT. A generic template is shown and explained with comments on what must be accomplished each week in the typical 26 week cycle. A real example is shown describing the special event, Dinner à la Heart, that was used as an example in the Introduction, and was planned for a longer cycle of 34 weeks plus 2 days. The METT's flexibility is illustrated in this example by showing it in reverse cycle from week 33 to week 1, plus the dinner week and dinner day, and dinner day plus 1.

Chapter 2 begins with a question: Should the organization even have an event? It contains a worksheet to help determine if the nonprofit can meet its goals. It then outlines the five types of special events and presents guidelines on how the nonprofit can make an intelligent choice based on its circumstances and the makeup of its constituencies. It completely describes how to use the METT, and integrates it with five key concepts that, once implemented, guide an organization to a successful special event.

Chapter 3 outlines and answers the financial questions that are an integral part of any fund-raising program, but especially for a special event. This chapter has eight exhibits: 3.1 is a sample revenue and expense budget; 3.2 is an example of how to price a special event; 3.3 describes the estimating attendance formula; 3.3a is an imput sheet for calculating the results of Exhibit 3.3, and is best utilized by loading into a spreadsheet application from the disk that comes with this book, inputting the numbers applicable to the special event, and then printing the results; 3.4 is an underwriters and sponsors matrix; 3.5 is an attendance matrix that uses the numbers from Exhibit 3.3a to generate a minimum reservation total; 3.6 is a list of database fields that the nonprofit can use to build a simple database for the special event; 3.7 shows the results of the database fields in a report form; and 3.8 is a list of revenue and expense budget line descriptions. The conclusion shows a refinement of METT, a subset of specific tasks to do for week 1.

Chapter 4 is a primer on how to recruit volunteer leadership for the special event. It describes the role and responsibilities of each event volunteer, from the chairperson and co-chairs to the community-wide committee members. This in-depth discussion leads to the Special Event Case Statement, a document that will enable the organization to recruit, with confidence, the lay leaders who will make the special event as successful as envisioned when the board first approached the project. There are six exhibits in this chapter: 4.1 is a graphic presentation and description of the responsibilities of the volunteers; 4.2 through 4.4 describe how to choose the lay leaders the board believes will best accomplish the job. Exhibit 4.2 is the macro list of potential candidates; through a filtering system and Exhibit 4.3 leads to the final "five-plus" acceptances. Exhibit 4.4 lists the result of Exhibits 4.2 and 4.3, the complete event executive cabinet. Exhibits 4.5 and 4.6 are checklists that keep track of the people who have volunteered to assist at the event.

Chapter 5 expands on the recruitment process through networking in the community. This chapter describes in detail the process of recruiting community members who will work for the nonprofit and make up the large general committee: the upfront workers. It goes into detail on how to set up and plan the one-and-only committee meeting. It shows examples of the committee invitation letter (Exhibit 5.1) and response card (Exhibit 5.2). The agenda for this vital meeting is shown in Exhibit 5.3. Exhibits 5.4 through 5.8 describe the documents each committee member receives at the meeting or by mail the next day; these documents, plus the marketing documents, make up the committee member's information kit (which can also be used as a media kit). A process is outlined on how to follow up with the committee members and how to motivate them. Chapter 5 concludes with comments and suggestions on how to manage the nonprofit's list of current, prospective, and immediate past donors, and offers a reminder about contacting potential corporate underwriters.

Chapter 6 is an overview on how to market the event. It details specific marketing methods that can be used to promote the event in a low-key way that will emphasize the event and the nonprofit without degrading the agency's mission and position in the community. This chapter also discusses the underwriting, sponsorship, and in-kind opportunities that the nonprofit can make available to individuals and businesses that fit into this category. Why discuss underwriting with marketing? Because they are opposite sides of the same coin! The discussion points out the many ramifications, pluses and minuses, to look for when soliciting this revenue. The chapter concludes with a detailed marketing and implementation plan designed specifically for special events.

Chapter 7 is the dot-the-*is*-and-cross-the-*t*s section dealing with logistics, all of those pesky little items that drive special event fund raisers up the wall. These include catering contracts; how to handle negotiations with the venue's catering manager; dealing with site managers on the proper staffing of the event; how to design the actual site for the optimum flow for dinners or receptions; working with the printer on layout, design, paper, and ink to use for invitations; and creating ad journals and the other event documents. How to take advantage of the post office's nonprofit rates, with specific document references cited, complete the chapter. The chapter has six exhibits. Exhibit 7.1 is a catering specification to use when soliciting bids for the event, whether it is a reception, breakfast, lunch, or dinner. Exhibit 7.2 is the table of honor design for award and testimonial dinners. Exhibits 7.3 through 7.6 are graphic designs for the most advantageous layout of a reception. Chapter 7 also includes a section on insurance and administrative financial matters for special events.

Chapter 8 is a countdown document entitled: "The Final Weeks to Event Day"! It outlines techniques to use in motivating the event chairs, committee members, and everyone else. It outlines a "hot" prospect scenario; Exhibit 8.1 is an example of a telephone script to use in calling event committee members. This chapter also delves into the mysteries of laying out the tables and seating guests for a sit-down meal event. The chapter finishes with examples of day-of-the-event documents, scripts, agendas, an overall timetable, and the people, documents, and queries (PDQ) checklist, a unique document that will not let the event planners forget anything!

Chapter 9 describes the big day, from what goes on from dawn until the last guest leaves the event. The chapter includes the usual check-off and responsibility lists (including an agency and site personnel list with telephone numbers) in Exhibit 9.1.

Chapter 10 discusses what goes on after the event is over. Subjects include: acknowledgments, thank-you letters, last-minute collections for unpaid reservations, and budget reconciliation. Exhibit 10.5 shows the important evaluation statement.

The resource section of the book is a special resource guide: A copy of the METT that will be used throughout; a guide to computer software programs and how to design an efficient but simple program of your own and a bibliography. The inside back cover contains a disk that includes all of the exhibits shown in this book formatted in Microsoft Word and Excel, MS Office '97 version.

Because computers are a big part of our working life, both Chapter 3 and the "Special Resource" section on computers and software explain how to use the computer effectively and economically when producing a special event. Depending on the agency's budget and computer skills, the organization can either purchase a specialized software program such as the Event Planner Plus™, a turnkey program designed by Certain Software for special event nonprofit fund raising, or it can purchase a database software program and design the reports needed. This section of Chapter 3 also illustrates sample reports that can be designed with an organization's own database program. Together, these items constitute a creative tool that can be used to sharpen ideas on how to produce the most profitable special event in the history of the agency.

CONCLUSION

An introduction to special events also introduces the reader to a unique fund-raising philosophy: Seven goals for successful special events. These goals point out the basic difference between a special event and other fund-raising programs: Special events reach more people at one time, introducing them to more opportunities to participate with the nonprofit. They also can, and many times do, initially cost more to raise a dollar, but—and this is a major but—the immediate and long term results can exceed a nonprofit's greatest expectations. The foundation laid in this introduction will support your plans for a special event if time is taken to consider what the nonprofit wants to achieve and then the time is spent to set up the mechanism to achieve those goals.

Remember, fund raising is an art not a science.

NOTES

[1] Rosso, *Achieving Excellence in Fund Raising* (San Francisco: Jossey-Bass, 1991).

[2] Grace, *Beyond Fund Raising* (New York: John Wiley & Sons, 1997).

[3] Mixer, *Principles of Professional Fundraising: Useful Foundations for Successful Practice* (San Francisco: Jossey-Bass, 1993).

CHAPTER ONE

The Master Event Timetable (METT)

THE MASTER EVENT TIMETABLE (METT)

The Master Event Timetable (METT) acts as a navigation guide throughout the special event planning process. It is the central document in this book. The minimum time line for the completion of a successful event is 26 weeks. When planning a community-wide extravaganza, festival, or a run or walk of any type, plan to schedule the event at least a year in advance.

This example of the METT is presented in a 27-week cycle: 26 weeks for planning the event and an extra week (always add this extra week; thus, a 39-week METT becomes 40 weeks, and the yearly planning METT becomes 53 weeks) for cleaning up loose ends, such as invoicing, completing reports, and mailing thank-you and acknowledgment letters (*very important*).

The METT is designed to "grow," for the more complex events by expanding the number of weeks for each task: For example, the METT shows planning and organization as first-week tasks. For a larger and more extensive event, planning and organization will take two to four weeks to complete and be approved by an agency's leadership committee (the development and/or executive committee, for example).

The worksheets, charts, tables, agendas, and other exhibits integrate with the METT to give a complete plan, start to finish. To use the book effectively, it is suggested that an agency integrate its own strategic overall development plan with the METT. The additional lines on the form will give an organization a complete picture of development activities (including the special event) throughout the year; it will be possible to sort out each segment—for example, the major gift campaign—whenever a snapshot of that activity is required.

A blank METT form is provided in the resource section and on the disk; information boxes indicate who is responsible, with a check-off box. It will guide the development committee through the event; completing the weekly tasks outlined in the METT will allow for planning of the agency's unique event. The METT links the key elements, tools, and chapters together. For example, week 1 in the METT outlines what should be accomplished to get the event started (key elements: planning and organization) and is described in detail in Chapter 1, along with the worksheets and documents required to complete the tasks for week 1.

Special event fund raising follows a careful time line, with a definite beginning and an end. A chronology of tasks to be completed, as shown in the METT, is essential for success—not to mention peace of mind. The METT can be designed for subsets of specific programs, such as the community event committee process: Start with week 9 and detail tasks, such as telephone follow-up before and after the meeting to make sure the committee member letters are mailed, and so on, through week 26.

Each chapter details an entire phase of the overall planning process. If this book has been purchased after the special event planning process has started, check the METT to determine the specific weekly status and begin at that point. Check progress by going back to week 1 to make sure the tasks have been completed. Always double-check every task, and document everything!

Make a copy of the METT and the completed worksheets and documents, and keep them in a binder (or create a computer binder with a software program) with numbered tabs corresponding to the week number. (Doing so also enables the agency to file chronologically related documents: letters, contracts, mailing lists, and press releases.)

The METT, Exhibit 1.1, can be modified for a particular event. A week by week explanation of the tasks will show the user how effective this tool can be for producing a successful special event. After this explanation, Exhibit 1.2 illustrates the METT with an actual example taken from Dinner à la Heart, described in the Introduction and shown in the countdown mode, for example, beginning with week 33 and ending with dinner day plus 1.

TO-DO THIS WEEK: THE METT IN ACTION

Week 1: Brings together all of the elements that are required to begin the strategic outline for a successful special event. Many of the elements have been discussed with the board, professional staff, and lay leaders prior to this formal beginning of the planning process. This is the week when the METT is prepared. Search begins for event site.

Week 2: This is the choose and recruitment week. Everyone peruses the list of potential leaders for the event and prepares a list of people that the event chairperson can recruit for the event team. The computer programming is set up; a software program is selected, or the agency uses existing database or spreadsheet programs to design their own programs (see examples in Chapter 3).

Week 3: Recruitment begins. A date, time, and place is selected for the initial meeting of the event chair and co-chairs. All recruited co-chairs are asked for a list of names which can be used to invite those people to join the event committee.

Week 4: Professional staff works with co-chair or committee member who has been recruited to act as the marketing and public relations specialist for the event; the marketing gurus assist in writing the press releases and save the date notices. First draft of invitation package is written.

Exhibit 1.1   Master Event Timetable (METT)
A Weekly Schedule of Tasks to Achieve a *Successful* Special Event

Week Number	To Do This Week	Responsible	☑
One	a) Governing board sets up Special Event Committee		
	b) Select Type of Special Event for your agency		
	c) Event Chairperson is recruited		
	d) Draft version of revenue & expense budget		
	e) Recruit Honoree and/or Special Guest(s)		
	f) Prepare Event time table		
	g) Update agency's Mission statement (if needed)		
	Set date & choose site for your event		
Two	a) Chairperson recruits co-chairs		
	b) Prepare preliminary list of prospective names for event committee and invitation list		
	c) Set up computer program		
Three	a) Recruit Honorary co-chairs		
	b) Complete co-chair recruitment		
	c) Set date for Event Chair & Co-Chair meeting		
	d) Obtain additional names from Chair & Co-Chairs		
Four	a) Establish marketing & public relations guidelines		
	b) Prepare press releases		
	c) Prepare Save the Date notices		
	d) Prepare draft of event invitation package		
Five	a) Agenda for event Chair & Co-Chairs meeting		
	b) Chair & Co-Chair to provide additional names for Event Committee		
	c) Set date for "one and only" Event Committee meeting		
	d) Discuss Other Sources of Revenue with Event Chair and co-Chairs		

(Continued)

Week Number	To Do This Week	Responsible	☑
Six	a) Start negotiations with site and catering managers		
	b) Continue recruiting committee members		
	c) Obtain insurance and governmental permits		
	d) Mail "Save the Date" notice to all names		
Seven	a) Select printer and mailing house		
	b) Determine size & layout of invitation package		
	c) Determine how many volunteers are required and outline their duties		
	d) Continue recruiting committee members through week 9		
	e) Work with ad journal co-chair and set-up solicitation campaign		
Eight	a) Prepare event committee information kits		
Nine	a) Mail Event Committee invitation letters		
Ten	a) Continue to add names to event invitation list through week 16		
Eleven ⇓	a) Start monoriting reservations from Dinner Committee mailing re: Budget ⇓		
Twelve ⇓	⇓		
Thirteen ⇓	⇓		
Fourteen ⇓	a) Event Committee meeting (one and only meeting)		
Fifteen	a) Telephone and/or Fax committee members and ask them to send their mailing lists to you ASAP!!		
Sixteen	a) Arrange site layout, sound, & decorating		
Seventeen	a) Complete in-kind solicitations		
Eighteen	a) Event invitations mailed		
	b) Follow up with event committee members and other prospects		
Nineteen	a) Event committee members mail personal letters to prospects		
Twenty	a) Prepare check list for items & people you need at event		

(Continued)

Exhibit 1.1 *(continued)*

Week Number	To Do This Week	Responsible	☑
Twenty-one	a) First deadline for ad journal copy; telephone all advertisers that have not submitted camera ready ad		
Twenty-two	a) Start FINAL PUSH telephone campaign for reservations and event journal ads		
Twenty-three	a) Final deadline for ad copy and camera ready material		
Twenty-four	a) Reconfirm all speaker and special guests arrangements		
Twenty-five	a) Bring everything altogether - You are almost there!		
Twenty-six	a) "EVENT DAY"		
Twenty-seven	a) Acknowledgments - Thank everyone involved!!		

Week 5: An agenda is prepared for the chair and co-chair meeting. Date, time, and place is set for the "one and only" community-wide event committee meeting. Staff begins discussions about other sources of revenue with chair and co-chairs.

Week 6: Absolutely the last week to find a site for the event. If site has been found and agreed upon, then negotiations with site catering manager take place. If needed, apply for insurance and other permits. Mail the "Save the Date" notice.

Week 7: Select printer and mailing house (if applicable); complete invitation design. Work with volunteer coordinator and determine how many are required and start to outline their duties.

Week 8: Staff begins preparations for community event committee meeting. Continue to recruit committee members.

Week 9: Mail community event committee invitation letters.

Week 10: Continue to gather names for the invitation list from committee members and lay leadership.

Week 11: Start monitoring reservation returns, advertisements, and donations received from community committee members.

Week 12: Continue week 11 activities.

Week 13: Continue week 11 and 12 activities.

Week 14: Community event committee's "one and only" meeting.

Week 15: Follow up with committee members re: invitation list.

Week 16: Work with site manager on physical event layout, sound and video, and decorations.

Week 17: Complete in-kind solicitations.

Exhibit 1.2   A Weekly Schedule for Dinner à la Heart

Week Number	To Do This Week	Responsible	☑
33 (7/1/97) ⇓⇓	Associates chairperson appoints event chairperson. Review and add names to prospective underwriters & sponsors. Review agency's mission statement; update if required. Determine where the event proceeds will be used; e.g., which agency program(s) will benefit. Prepare underwriting & sponsor letter; have assigned committee members personally sign their letters & mail. Begin to recruit new committee members. Prepare time line. Draft budget projections. Recruit co-chairpersons.	Associates & Dinner à la Heart Chairpersons Committee Chairs & Staff	
24 (8/29/97)			
23 (9/1/97) ⇓	Chairperson meets with committee co-chairs and professional staff to outline responsibilities. Save the date; draft most forms required; give to designer. Update and expand mailing lists. Update restaurant list; prepare information packets for solicitors. Begin restaurant solicitations. Begin in-kind solicitations.		
19 (10/3/97)	Begin marketing & public relations contacts (many publications require a minimum of four months lead time for calendar items).		
15 (10/31/97)	Complete corporate underwriting and sponsorship solicitations.		
14 (11/2/97)	Complete restaurant solicitations, & acknowledge.		
11 (11/28/97)	Finalize & approve advertising schedule & budget.		
10 (12/1/97) to	Finalize restaurant recruitment; obtain signed contracts. Complete invitation package: restaurant card, personal notes from solicitors, and mail on December 29, 1997.		
6 (12/31/97)	Establish procedure for restaurant income and payments with accounting department.		
5 (1/5/98)	Begin to accept guest reservations; Monday, January 5, 1998.		

(Continued)

Exhibit 1.2 *(continued)*

Week Number	To Do This Week	Responsible	☑
⇓	Print table tents for restaurants.		
⇓	Assign host & hostesses for each restaurant; mail instructions; prepare checklist for Dinner Day.		
2 (1/30/98)	Mail reminder letter to restaurant (week three and/or two).		
1 (2/2/98)	Finalize guest reservations.		
	Deliver to restaurant: list of attendees & name of host/hostess.		
Dinner Week (2/9/98)	Complete checklist items.		
Dinner Day	TUESDAY, FEBRUARY 10, 1998 Deliver to each restaurant: centerpieces, table tents, and favors.		
Dinner Day Plus 1	Pay restaurants; include thank-you note, within two days after the event.		
	Evaluate event & make recommendations for next year.		
	Complete financial report for board and accounting department.		

Week 18: Event invitation mailed. Continue to work with committee members re: reservations.

Week 19: Last week for committee members to mail personal invitation letters to prospects.

Week 20: Prepare PDQ checklist.

Week 21: Deadline week for ad and camera ready copy.

Week 22: Begin final push for reservations.

Week 23: Continue work of weeks 21 and 22.

Week 24: Reconfirm arrangements for speakers and entertainment.

Week 25: Confirm all pending reservations and obtain names from table purchasers.

Week 26: **EVENT DAY**

Week 27: Thank you and goodbye! Acknowledgements.

MASTER EVENT TIMETABLE APPLIED
TO DINNER À LA HEART

The time line for Dinner à la Heart moves at a steady pace, with the planning and goal-setting process beginning approximately seven and one-half months prior to event day. Thirty-three week's planning for a mostly volunteer-oriented event is realistic. In Exhibit 1.1 the generic METT is shown as a 26-week timetable; this example shows how flexible the METT can be, it can be expanded or contracted with ease. Its weekly segments can also be displayed in reverse, which is often referred to as the "countdown" mode (as the Dinner à la Heart example is shown).

METT Checklist for Chapter 1

Week 1	To Do This Week	Book Ref.	☑
a)	Draft a version of the METT on the computer; as event and meeting dates, and recruitment of volunteers become final, fill in the information and print a current copy for everyone who needs to know: event volunteers and professional and support staff.	Chp. 1	

CONCLUSION

The METT is the basic guide through the special event forest. It prevents the reader from experiencing the old cliché: You cannot see the trees because of the forest!

The tasks listed in the generic METT can be added to and refined, to meet the requirements of a nonprofit's particular special event. As shown, the METT is flexible and can be outlined as a subset for each specific task.

Every hour spent detailing the special event tasks can save the nonprofit professional or volunteer almost a day of frustration. Remember—fundraising is an art, not a science.

CHAPTER TWO

Choosing the Event

DO NOT PASS GO—SHOULD THE ORGANIZATION HAVE AN EVENT?

Exhibit 2.1 (🔒CH0201.DOC) shows hypothetical criteria that a non-profit organization should consider when determining whether it should produce a special event. The Special Event Goals in the left-hand column are the seven bedrock goals described in Chapter 1. When those goals are related to the columns Current Situation, Require Now, and Future Needs, they give the nonprofit a blueprint of its current fund-raising situation to determine how implementing a special event might help it achieve the desired result. If the nonprofit decides to implement the event, it also can use the chart to plan a future development strategy using the Future Needs column, which lists goals to help choose the type of special event that will best achieve the desired results. By applying the techniques described in the following chapters, an agency will be able to evaluate intelligently the immediate fiscal year as well as future years. The case statement described in Chapter 4 will enable lay leaders to assemble concrete information to present to potential volunteers and contributors. A word of warning: Do not fall into the let-them-know-only-what-they-need-to-know trap. Planning and strategizing for special events and for any nonprofit fund-raising program is not an atomic secret that must be kept hidden by a nonprofit CIA.

Exhibit 2.2 (🔒CH0202.DOC) Special Event Resource Worksheet, measures the nonprofit's available resources that will enable it to either produce, or not to put on a special event. The decision is an intuitive one, the professional staff must feel comfortable with the positive resources of the agency when it decides to go forward and produce the event.

The agency's staff's time availability per week, measured in full time equivalents (FTEs) is crucial.

The volunteer base is vital for a successful event. This base includes the agency's board of directors, and as indicated in the worksheet, they must be willing to support the event; they should have some connections with the communities hierarchy in the corporate, political, and social world. And, most importantly, they should be willing to network and recruit their friends and colleagues to serve on the volunteer committee and support the event financially. Finally, the agency must have financial resources to provide "front money" to fund initial expenses until funds start coming in from the event.

KEY ELEMENTS FOR EXECUTING A SPECIAL EVENT

There are four key elements that define the structure of a special event: *goal setting, planning, organization,* and *administration.* An analogy that

Exhibit 2.1   Determining Special Event Goals for the Nonprofit Organization

Special Event Goals	Current Situation	Require Now	Future Needs
•MONEY	Fund Raising = $80,000	$100,500 to meet budget	$150,000 in two years
•MOTIVATION	10 of 25 board members active	20 out of 25 active	25 active board members
•VOLUNTEER RECRUITMENT	35 active volunteers	60 active volunteers	100 active volunteers
•EXPAND THE NETWORK	1,500 names on donor & prospect list	2,500 names	3,500 to 5,000 names
•MONEY	750 active donors	1,250 active donors	2,000-plus active donors
•MARKETING	Local name recognition	County-wide name recognition	Metropolitan area name recognition
•MISSION STATEMENT & MARKETING	Limited programming— one location	Multiple county location programming	Metropolitan area programming sites
•SOLICIT ENDORSEMENTS	Very few	Corporate and local government recognition	State & areawide recognition from overall community

Exhibit 2.2   Special Event Resource Worksheet

Agency's Resources	Y/N	Number
Agency's time availability for special event—per week—FTEs (1/4, 1/3, 1/2, 3/4, 1/1)		
Does the agency have a volunteer base? Approximate number of volunteers.		
Does the agency have monetary reserves to provide up-front money for the special event? How much money can it provide?		
Are the agency's board and major supporters willing to provide backing for the event?		
Are board members represented in the community's political, social, and corporate world?		
Will the board members and other supporters network with their colleagues?		
Will board members take an active role in the event hierarchy?		

would explain how these element relate to the event would be the seven goals described in the Introduction as being the foundation of a building that needs support for its four sides; the four key elements being the four sides and infrastructure of the building. The special event flows from this house, using the METT as its guide, as soon as the agency decides to produce one, and then the event becomes an integral part of the agency's development plan.

Before choosing an event type, think of the big picture; determining the flow of any project lets a person see the endeavor from the beginning to the conclusion. Continue along with this book to assimilate its philosophy and to learn that the completed special event is, in fact, just the beginning of the donor stewardship process. Based on the four elements, the following "need-to-do" list should be in the decision makers' minds as they choose an event:

Need-to-Do List

GOAL SETTING

1. Set the monetary goal for the special event.
2. Estimate attendance at the special event.
3. Construct a realistic budget for the event. Building revenue sources is the most important task of budgeting for a special event.

PLANNING

1. Revisit the mission statement; bring it up to date; if necessary, rewrite it in understandable words that clarify what the agency is accomplishing in the community.

   a. Determine who in the leadership structure (from the board, executive, or development committee) will take responsibility for this event. (See "Tactics" subparagraph c.)

   b. Strategy, when it relates to special events, means that specific programs are used to complete the event: Preparing the budget, choosing the event leadership, and getting them involved are part of the total event strategy.

   c. Tactics, as they relate to nonprofit fund raising, are simply stated: Involve volunteer supporters. This is accomplished by defining their responsibilities and how the agency will assist them in fulfilling their duties. (See Chapter 4.)

   d. A time line is essential to achieve goals; see Introduction section and the METT.

    e.   Define the agency's natural and community constituency; who will be targeted for this event? How will names and addresses of prospects to contact be found? (See Chapters 4 and 5.)

ORGANIZING

1. Recruit the special event leadership and committee members. (See Chapter 4.)
2. Don't forget to involve current, past, and prospective supporters.
3. Recruit and learn how to use honorary leaders.
4. Set event chair and co-chair's meeting agenda.
5. Set the one (and only) community event committee meeting.

ADMINISTRATION

1. See Chapter 9 and the PDQ checklist for a list of required documents.
2. There are many contracts to consider: Hotel and catering, insurance, printing, entertainment, e.g., orchestra, and celebrities (have your attorney read these contracts before signing), items donated for auctions, and vendors' contracts.
3. An insurance policy to protect against accidents is a basic necessity.
4. Printing requirements need to be planned and scheduled, especially if there is an ad journal involved.
5. Ambiance is not strictly an administration item, but it needs to be considered if the event is to achieve the outlined goals. Just the addition of flowers at an event can raise the ambiance level and make the event a warm, friendly affair.
6. Computer software, either your in-house or off-the-shelf program must be in place at the same time the METT is drafted.

A condensed listing of these elements can be found in Exhibit 2.3 (CH0203.DOC) and on the disk.

CHOOSING A SPECIAL EVENT

Special event fund-raising programs target the nonprofit's natural constituency. Using these supporters and prospects as a base, the next step is to build a network and add prospects from the other members of an

Exhibit 2.3   Key Elements for a Special Event
How to structure a special event to achieve maximum success

Goals

1. Raise *funds*.
2. Revisit your *mission* statement.
3. *Motivate* volunteers.
4. *Recruit* additional volunteers.
5. *Networking:* Expand the natural constituency.
6. *Market* the agency.

Planning

1. Draft a Master Event Timetable (METT).
2. Write a *strategic* plan for this special event.
   a. Amount of funds organization wants to raise; how and from whom?
3. Specify *responsibilities* for event leadership.
4. Write a *tactical* plan for utilization of volunteers.
5. Construct an event *budget*.
6. Develop a specific *marketing* plan for your event.

Organization

1. Define *committees* for the event.
2. *Recruit* committee members.
   a. Current contributors
   b. Past contributors
   c. Prospects
   d. Honorary members: past honorees, political and prominent community leaders

Administration

1. Documents
2. Contracts
3. Insurance
4. Printing
5. Ambiance
6. Computer Software

organization's constituency and then the entire community. Chapter 4 describes in detail how this can be accomplished.

At this point, the adage of "Don't put all your eggs in one basket" is apt, particularly as it relates to nonprofit fund raising. One point must be emphasized and explained: A special event is one of many programs in a nonprofit's development plan and should not be considered as a stand-alone fund-raising vehicle that makes other fund-raising programs unnecessary. In fact, special events should be looked at as a feeder river flowing to the larger bay of fund-raising programs. Do not rely on special events or any other fund-raising program to do the entire job for an agency; as in real life, teamwork and planning are the keys to opening up the door to raising funds.

How should a nonprofit choose a special event? First, let us describe what an agency should *not* do. Let us assume that a sister organization whose program is similar to an agency's has been producing a special event that features well-known celebrities performing in concert to sell-out audiences at the local auditorium. An agency—specifically, its board of directors—is envious. Many board meetings are devoted to the why-can't-we-do-this? pleas of board members; the executive director is questioned ad nauseum, and in turn begins questioning the development director to transfer the challenge to that person. Do not let an organization fall into this trap. An organization should evaluate its own resources and goals to determine if it is ready for a special event and then make an intelligent choice based only on those factors.

Use Exhibit 2.4 (📀 CH0204.DOC), Choosing a Special Event, in conjunction with Exhibit 2.2, Agency Resources, to help choose the best event for an agency. In some cases, doing this will lead to the decision *not* to produce a special event until adequate resources are available. Although arbitrary, using an agency's budget size gives information on how many resources it might be able to muster to produce a special event. For example, an agency with a budget of less than $2,000,000 probably will have a difficult time producing a community-wide event because of staff size and the time involved to produce such an event. An agency would have to devote one staff person for an average of at least one-third FTE per week to produce a community-wide event. Until it secures an underwriter for the event, the agency would probably have to provide up-front funds of $10,000 to $30,000. Thus, many larger agencies would have a difficult time providing this amount of money, as cash flow is usually very tight at nonprofits.

Exhibit 2.4   Choosing a Special Event

Agency's Annual Budget (in thousands)	Community-Wide Events	Auctions	Parties	Tournaments	Testimonials
$100 TO $250					
$250 TO $500					
$500 TO $750					
$750 TO $1,000					
$1,000 TO $1,500					
$1,500 TO $2,500					
OVER $2,500					

FIVE MODELS FOR A SPECIAL EVENT

1. Community-wide special events
2. Auctions
3. Theater and art gallery opening parties
4. Sporting events, such as golf and tennis tournaments
5. Testimonial events: Award or tribute dinners

Many branches can sprout from these models; a nonprofit should be creative and tailor the event for its active supporters and the community as a whole. The following text outlines these popular types of special events. (A worksheet is provided in Exhibit 2.4 and on the disk to aid in the decision-making process.) Goal references refer to a specific goal of the seven goals explained in the Introduction.

Community-Wide Special Events

Community-wide special events are designed to involve thousands of people in an activity such as a run or walk around the town. The entry price is low—usually no more than $15 to $25. After the race there is usually a food, goods, and entertainment fair where manufacturers and service companies give away and/or sell their products to the race participants and the general public, and where everyone can enjoy free entertainment. These events succeed because the nonprofit has obtained sponsorship underwriting from an organization that will pay for the "for-profit" commercial event-planning company that the nonprofit employs to produce and run the event (with the help of the nonprofit's volunteers). In return for the underwriting fee, the sponsoring organization receives media and other forms of recognition, for example, "The XYZ Corporation and ABC Charities bring you the 'Around-the-Town Run and Walk—Food and Products fair.' "

This is not an event for the timid, however. But by gaining access to monetary and people resources, a nonprofit can achieve many of the goals that define a special event, especially raising a large amount of money at one time. The various metropolitan marathons (Boston and New York) and the San Francisco Bay to Breakers race are examples of this type of community-wide special event. Smaller-scale community-wide events like this take place almost every week throughout the year, but even those require numerous volunteers and usually a commercial events company to run the event.

Exhibit 2.5   Community-Wide Special Event: ADL Annual Dinner Dance Invitation

The Anti-Defamation League
cordially requests the pleasure of your company
at its

Annual Dinner Dance
Sunday, November 17, 1996
The Fairmont Hotel, San Francisco

FEATURING
Theodore Bikel
BACK BY POPULAR DEMAND!

5:30 p.m. Cocktails   6:15 p.m. Dinner   Cocktail Attire   RSVP enclosed

Used with permission from Anti-Defamation League.

Advantages: The agency has wide exposure to the community, which means excellent public relations opportunities. If managed correctly, it is a good moneymaker and a fun way to recruit volunteers, some of whom will help with other projects. (Goals: 1. Raise Money; 4. Volunteer recruitment; 6. Marketing)

Cautions: An agency must have many volunteers; such a program is very labor- and time-intensive.

Auctions

Auctions are very popular nonprofit special events. (See Exhibit 2.6 for an invitation.) They can be successful with only 150 to 300 bidders and have the added feature of flexibility of venue: An auction can be held as its own stand-alone event or be combined with another event, such as an awards dinner or sports event. A main feature and bonus of an auction is that agency volunteers usually can obtain donations of goods, services, and merchandise from various merchants and suppliers. Hence, event expenses are low relative to gross revenue, and the net income is greater. The donors receive recognition in the auction book and from the auctioneer when he or she gavels the item. They also receive a tax write-off based on the wholesale price. (Check with the IRS for the current regulations).

Two types of auctions are possible: silent and live. The silent auction is held during the cocktail reception prior to the live auction event. The silent auction is for those items that can be placed on tables and have economical price tags. The higher-priced items are always held for the live auction. Silent auctions also are used in combination with an awards dinner or sports tournament. As the name implies, silent auctions are conducted without live bidding. Bidders walk around the room and stop at the tables that interest them. On the tables, in front of each item is a "bid" sheet on which they can enter their bid and name. Silent bidding is a timed event, which usually ends just prior to the beginning of the live auction. About 20 minutes before the announced time, bidders are warned. The warning is repeated every 5 or 8 minutes until the actual cut-off time. The bidding sheets then are collected and the high bidder wins.

Auctions are labor-intensive and require two types of volunteers: people who have a large circle of friends and acquaintances who can be asked for donations of merchandise, services, and goods; and volunteers who are reliable and can help at the actual auction with the many details of recording, redeeming, and taking the money for the items purchased.

Exhibit 2.6   Auction: ADL Annual Auction Invitation

You are cordially invited to attend

the

ADL

on

Sunday, March 15, 1998

Westin St. Francis
335 Powell Street
San Francisco

5:30 p.m.	Cocktails & Silent Auction	Couvert $150 per person
7:00 p.m.	Buffet	Informal Attire
8:30 p.m.	Program & Live Auction	RSVP enclosed

Used with permission from Anti-Defamation League.

A popular event is an ethnic food pavilion, a dance, and an auction. A nonprofit can charge a nominal amount to cover the cost of food and beverages. The combination of food, dance, and good wine plays well with a fund-raising event that is disguised as an auction. Some favorite auction items are: dinner for two at the best restaurants in the community; sports memorabilia (signed baseballs and footballs and T-shirts); rare and "good"-year wines, either by the bottle or by the case; rare automobiles (but only as an outright gift or on consignment with a minimum bid that is well publicized in advance); tickets to sporting events, concerts, plays, and movies; and vacation trips (check with the community's largest travel agency). Items to be leery of: paintings (unless the artist is recognized by everyone); books (even the rare ones); clothing; unknown or outdated computer hardware and software (but new or nearly new computers and electronic items are very popular).

Advantages: Auctions have the potential for good net revenue; they are flexible programs that can be integrated with other special events. Volunteers like auctions because of their scavenger-hunt aspect; they find it easier to ask for a donation of goods or services than to ask for money. (Goals: 1. Raise Money; 3. Motivation)

Cautions: Auctions are labor-intensive; volunteers sometimes get too enthusiastic and will accept anything for the auction. Beware of other people's "white elephants" (especially artwork).

Theater and Art Gallery Opening Parties

Theater and gallery and other "opening" parties are popular because they are easy to produce. The hook used to draw people to the event is built in: a new movie with popular stars (who will attend the opening, it is hoped), an opportunity to meet the artist and buy his or her work directly (and perhaps have a picture taken with him or her). The point is, these events are fun, are usually reasonably priced, and, depending on the site, can draw lots of people. The nonprofit can make some money as well as achieve some other goals, including public relations and adding prospects to the donor list. However, a successful event still requires organization and planning and support of the nonprofit's board of directors.

Advantages: Openings are easy to produce. They usually make a profit. They present the agency in an informal setting. (Goals: 1. Raise Money; 5. Expand Your Network)

Cautions: Openings require total agency board support, which is sometimes hard to organize; "stars" often do not show up at openings.

Sporting Events

Sport tournaments, like golf, tennis, and bowling, are popular fund-raising events held at various athletic clubs where the members are part of the agency's natural constituency, as seen in Exhibit 2.7. The club usually sets aside certain days that are traditionally slow for use by non-profit agencies so that the club can keep its facilities fully staffed. Make sure that the club does not discriminate and adheres to the antidiscrimination laws. Plan an event that will draw prospects who are not members and want to take advantage of using the club, especially if it is an outstanding club, with facilities to match. These events are not labor-intensive and can be run by the nonprofit's staff; the food service can be run by the club's catering department. Depending on the arrangements made with the club, it is possible to show a reasonable net income. The agency also can hold a raffle of donated merchandise to raise a few more dollars. The main idea behind these events is to have fun while raising money and consciousness for and about an agency.

Advantages: If an agency has a large sports-oriented constituency, such an event can achieve great results; it also works well as a "society" type of event. (Goals: 1. Raise money; 3. Motivation; 6. Market the nonprofit)

Cautions: An agency must have large support base whose members belong to the country club set, or this event will fall on its face. Furthermore, it can be labor-intensive, so a strong staff and a core group of sports-minded volunteers are needed.

Testimonial Events

Testimonial events cover two main types of special events: award and tribute dinners and many variants, such as theme dinners and dinner dances, as seen in Exhibits 2.5 and 2.8. Testimonial events are considered the "granddaddy" of special events since they date back to antiquity. Today, they are still the most popular type of special event. There is a subtle difference between tribute and award events: Tribute events are produced by nonprofits to honor one of their own outstanding leaders; award events honor an outstanding community, professional, or corporate executive who has given his or her time and usually money to fund programs to improve community institutions.

Theme dinner events can be award or tribute events, honoring a person from the own agency or someone on the outside who has been active in the community. The dinner is connected to the honoree's

Exhibit 2.7   S. F. Giants Annual Community Fund Golf Classic Tournament

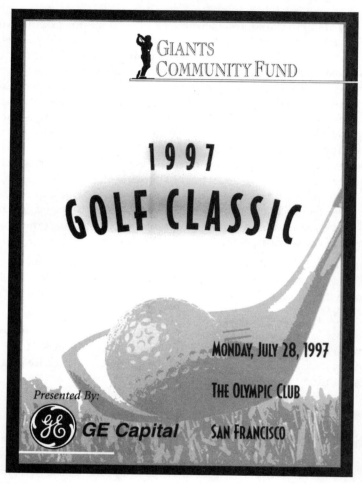

(A)

Used with permission from Giants Community Fund and GE Capital.

industry or special interests. For example, Northern California's Napa Valley is home to one of most interesting industries in the world, the growing of grapes and making of fine wines. Located about 75 miles from San Francisco, many nonprofits hold black-tie events at the Napa Valley wineries that draw 300 to 500 people from San Francisco at prices that usually start at $250 per person. They usually honor a person connected to the wine industry. If the honoree is affiliated with the agency as an active supporter, the event is a tribute dinner. If the hon-

Exhibit 2.7 *(continued)*

Join us at
THE OLYMPIC CLUB IN SAN FRANCISCO
on
MONDAY, JULY 28, 1997

Tournament Schedule

9:15 am
  - Registration
  - Continental breakfast with Giants celebrities
  - Driving range and putting green open for practice

10:30 am   Shotgun start

Lunch on Course

Evening Festivities
· Hosted Reception with Giants celebrities
· Dinner and Awards Ceremony
· Sports Memorabilia Auction and Raffle

Special Features
· Photo of foursome with your celebrity player
· Golf awards for winners on each course
· Tee prizes including special collectibles from the Giants and The Olympic Club

(B)

Used with permission from Giants Community Fund and GE Capital.

oree is a community "asset" and supports many nonprofits, then it is an awards dinner. In either case, it is a theme event.

Another example is to honor a person from a distinctive ethnic background and serve ethnic food and entertain the guests with ethnic dancing and music.

The types of theme events are almost endless, and can focus on a number of professions, including, attorneys, physicians, businesspersons, and CPAs.

Exhibit 2.8   ADL Torch of Liberty Testimonial Award Dinner Dance

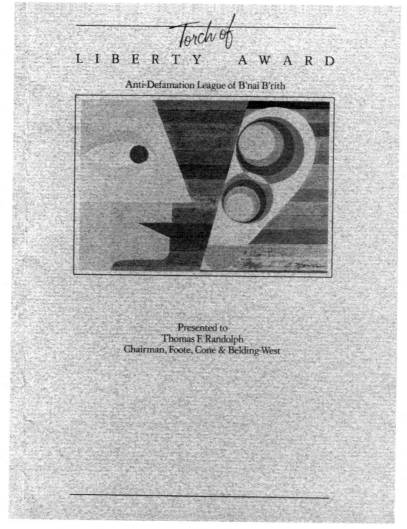

(A)

Used with permission from Anti-Defamation League.

Important Hint

An agency's reputation must be kept in the forefront at all times:
Always honor a deserving person and/or organization, and produce
an event that the agency will be proud of!

Dinner dances are celebratory types of events typically held as trib-
utes to an in-house person at the agency's annual get-together; often

Exhibit 2.8 *(continued)*

The honor of your presence is cordially requested

at the

Torch of Liberty Award Dinner-Dance

of the

Anti-Defamation League of B'nai B'rith

honoring

THOMAS F. RANDOLPH

Chairman, Foote, Cone & Belding-West

at a dinner in his honor

Wednesday, April 16, 1986

Fairmont Hotel — Gold Room
Atop Nob Hill

San Francisco

D I N N E R   C H A I R M E N

Lee Bartlett	Ray Barnett
Chairman,	Vice President,
Cole & Weber-California	General Manager *KCBS*
Reception at Half Past Six	$250 Per Person
Dinner at Half Past Seven	$2500 Table of Ten
Black Tie Optional	R.S.V.P.
No Solicitation of Funds	

(B)

Used with permission from Anti-Defamation League.

they feature vocalists, comics, and choral groups. (See Exhibit 2.5.) Generally, the price of admission is established by the amount of the donor's annual gift. It is considered a thank-you event for the annual donor and sometimes is linked with postevent solicitations to upgrade givers to a higher level and to encourage them to become more active with the nonprofit. Annual supporters are encouraged to bring friends to dinner–

dance events in hopes of getting them interested in supporting the nonprofit.

Advantages: These events can achieve all of the seven goals a special event is designed for, from spotlighting the agency in the community to creating an opportunity for the agency to present its mission statement and values to the community; and it is also a good moneymaker!

Cautions: The ease of producing this type of special event can be narcotic if overdone. An agency cannot force an event on the community; otherwise, it will lose support from existing donors and supporters.

EMERGENCY DRILL

The following is a true story, with the names changed, of course. Alpha nonprofit's president, Laura, had just started to tell Eddie, the executive director, an experience she had had at TGI's recent awards dinner, when Mark Maven, Alpha's fund-raising consultant, walked in for the scheduled meeting. "Mark, I want you to hear this," Laura said, "I attended TGI's awards dinner last week for two reasons: First, my partner Ben Megabucks was the honoree and, second, I wanted to experience it with a critical eye, since we are planning to produce a testimonial event. Of course, in the past few years I have attended many such events, and as a guest I have just let the evening flow along and did not pay any attention to the mechanics of the dinner. Recently, unless they are special, like TGI's, I have avoided them and have supported the cause with a contribution instead. Since I'm going to be involved with ours, I thought I had better bring myself up to date."

"Did you achieve your objectives?" asked Mark.

At this point, Laura sat down and indicated that Mark and Eddie should do the same. From the look on her face, all had not gone well at TGI's award dinner. Laura started: "The first part of the evening—the check-in table and the reception—went very well, and we were seated on time. After the welcome, and just as we were about to eat our salad, it started raining! The dinner was held inside in the Hotel Elegance's grand ballroom. The grand ballroom is located two floors below the main lobby where the largest indoor fountain in the state is located. The fountain is situated directly above the ballroom, and it started to overflow; before the engineers could fix the broken valve, it rained on Ben Megabuck's parade. Four tables were wiped out and almost all of the 40 people involved got wet, some of them *very* wet. The hotel staff ran around like chickens with their heads cut off. The dinner captain was frozen in place with no clue as to what he should do. If it weren't for Norm Goodguy, the dinner's event chair, everyone would have headed for the exits. Norm quickly borrowed an umbrella, went to the podium, and led us in his version of 'Singing in the Rain.' There were many ugly moments, which would take another hour to relate; the event never really recovered and went downhill from there. Is there planning that we can do to avoid a disaster like this at our event?"

Mark said, "Yes, up to a certain point. We can make contingency plans to avoid the ineptitude of the hotel staff. However, the hotel's fountain problems can be avoided only by not holding an event there, until it has new plumbing installed. Seriously, I think TGI was very fortunate to have Norm Goodguy as its chair. Most other chairs would have also frozen like the hotel staff, and then there would have been a real nasty disaster. Wet, hungry guests can become very unfriendly, and nothing can keep them from telling all of their friends and business associates.

"On another level, the hotel is fully insured and the agency should have all its out-of-pocket expenses, plus damages for a ruined marketing effort, taken care of. What advance plans should we make to avoid catering-staff paralysis? First, Alpha's staff and the dinner chairs should have a card listing all the hotel's catering managers' and food and beverage directors' direct telephone numbers and home numbers if possible, as well as names of front desk managers who will be on duty that night, with their phone extensions. Second, we should have the head housekeeper's representative's name and number; housekeeping is the source of clean towels and bathrobes and also can probably send someone to iron the wet clothing (which TGI really needed.) Last, a staff member should be seated at every table so that any emergency can be handled by a trained professional."

METT Checklist for Chapter 2

Week 1	To Do This Week	Book Ref.	✓
a)	Key Elements provides a guide for establishing sequence of activities. The type, date, and time of the event must be chosen this week. Chapter 2 provides tools that will let the nonprofit accomplish this task.		
2 a)	Computer program should be "up and running."		

CONCLUSION

Chapter 2 has taken you through a decision process that helps the non-profit decide on whether they want to produce a special event to the type of event that would be best for them to hold. We have provided a Key Elements list of items that must be accomplished to achieve most of the Seven Goal philosophy, which in turn will result in a successful event. Anticipate problems to minimize a special event disaster!

CHAPTER THREE

Monetary Goals and Budgets

INTRODUCTION

A special event budget is a financial and planning statement that allocates anticipated revenue to pay for expenses. Logically, budget planning comes between strategic planning for the event and organizing your working committees. During this interval, many nonprofits try to avoid the process of calculating detailed revenue and expense items by estimating a gross and net revenue figure. This method of calculating revenue and expense from out of the thin air is dangerous for two reasons: One, the nonprofit has no idea about the relationship between the two figures, and two, revenue is left on the "table" because the agency has not thought about the many sources of funds that can be solicited for a special event.

Budgets are drawn up before networking and organizing the event committee in order to facilitate recruitment of chair and committee persons. Signing on the most effective committee chair and members for a special event is so important that a case must be made to convince these people that the agency has "dotted the i's and crossed the t's." Prominent doers receive more requests to chair events than they can respond to, so they need to see a logical plan and a realistic budget to be convinced that an event strategy is doable. By using these financial tools, the nonprofit is showing the lay leader how organized the agency is and how much thought and planning has been given to make the event a success. Everyone likes to be associated with success. (The recruitment process is discussed in detail in Chapter 4, as is the case statement for special events.)

This chapter begins with a detailed list of the many sources of revenue a typical special event can produce. It will then go on to look at expenses, and the concluding section of the chapter involves the use of computer software and the help that can result from its use. A staff person with a good understanding of computer software can achieve a great deal of results in the administration of the event. There are exhibits in this section that will guide the event planner and save him or her a lot of time.

KEY ELEMENTS TO CONSIDER WHEN PUTTING TOGETHER THE SPECIAL EVENT

The following key elements lead the event planners—the event committee and the professional staff—through a logical strategy based on the Seven Goals for Special Events discussed in the Introduction. Goal one is raising money (completed events can be considered successes when approximately two-thirds of the collected revenues remain in the nonprofit's bank account after all expenses have been paid), but the other six goals concentrate on people, either motivating them, or recruiting them to work for the agency. Even the interpretation of the Mission Statement and the Marketing of the nonprofit involve people as their end result.

1. Budget strategy
2. Calculating revenue sources from seat, table, and ad journal sales
3. Estimating attendance: Calculating minimum revenue from estimated guest attendance
4. Other sources of revenue
5. Underwriters and sponsors
6. What items make up gross revenue: Income from guest reservations, advertisements in event journal, packaging advertisements and table sales, donations, underwriters and sponsors income, and in-kind gifts
7. Mastering revenue and expense items
8. Computer spreadsheets and databases: How these tools can help you keep the event and the budget on track

This chapter considers each of these points in turn.

BUDGET STRATEGY

A budget is a strategic and crucial element of all fund-raising programs. Special events require financial monitoring from week 1, so planners can check on a regular basis and compare revenue and expense amounts to make sure the income and outgo are within the budgeted figures. Expenses start within the first few weeks after the decision is made to produce a special event. Revenue begins after the first letter to the event committee is mailed, usually week 9. (See the METT.) This is why the METT is so important; it not only keeps the event on track, it links the timetable tasks with the budget income and expense. When these strategic documents are completed, the agency will know the size and complexity of the special event it is producing. If the money bite is too large for the agency's cash flow, and the staff and lay leaders feel overwhelmed, the project should be pared down; likewise, if the event planners have been extremely cautious, then it is not too late to expand to a more reasonable size.

Successful nonprofits are bottom line–oriented in regard to fund raising. The board of directors requires answers to basic questions: How much is the organization going to raise? How much will it cost to raise that amount? The board also demands to see a detailed plan committed to paper that will answer these questions. When a plan involves special events, it should be clear and conservative. Why? Because of the up-front money that is required to produce a special event: Deposits for hotels and/or sites, caterers, printing, and postage. If special events are not a regular activity for an agency, then the staff time devoted to this project, including training of support personnel, must be considered. The event consultant should plan a presentation to give to the executive committee to discuss and address these questions. A rational determination must be made before the agency goes forward with the event. If the agency asks itself some logical questions, designing the budget will be a welcome step in the planning process and not the bane of special event planning.

The revenue and expense budget seen in Exhibit 3.1 (CH0301.XLS) is designed for a testimonial event and is provided because this type of event is very popular with many nonprofits; it also offers an example of varied revenue and expense lines. (Later this chapter provides an extensive list of revenue and expense categories that will cover most special events and will assist planning committee members when they discuss a potential event—that is, when they put pencil to paper when they plan the initial financial parameters of an event.)

Dollar amounts cannot be placed opposite budget line items until there is a concept of what the agency is trying to accomplish. In the Introduction and Chapter 2, special event goals and objectives were defined and the types of events were illustrated. After completing the Chapter 2 worksheets, the line items for revenue and expense can be inserted into the budget. For example, if an event is held at a site other than a hotel or facility where the food service is available, then catering and site costs plus a dozen different expense items must be brought into the budget mix.

Finally, remember that every event is different. No two are identical, even those that are given year after year, with essentially the same audience. New budget lines will always be required because someone has thought of a new idea to make the event more of a gala or to draw more people.

Event Pricing

Before building a budget, or even projecting a revenue figure, the dollar figures must be established for individual and full table seat reservations. The basic price per seat is used as a base for pricing the

Exhibit 3.1 Revenue and Expense Budget Items

	A	B	C	D	E	F	G	H
1								
2								
3								
4	REVENUE SOURCES:						Percentage of total revenue	
5							⇓	
6	Individual Reservations:		450 × $150			$67,500.00	67.16%	
7								
8	Premium Tables:							
9		Gold:	(20 × $250)			$5,000.00	4.98%	
10		Silver:	(50 × $200)			$10,000.00	9.95%	
11								
12	Donations:	(3% of $100,000)				$3,000.00	2.99%	
13								
14	Ad Journal:	(10% of $100,000)				$10,000.00	9.95%	
15	Sum Cash Items:					$95,500.00		
16	In-Kind:	(5% of $100,000)				$5,000.00	4.98%	
17								
18	TOTAL REVENUE:					$100,500.00	100.00%	
19								
20								
21	EXPENSES:	Percentage of expense divided by total revenue						
22							⇓	
23	Food: (520 People × $45)					$23,400.00	23.28%	
24								
25	Beverage:(100 bottles/wine @$14)					$1,400.00	1.39%	
26								
27	Corkage:(only if wine is donated)							
28								
29	Postage:(2000 pieces × $0.32)					$640.00	0.64%	
30								
31	Printing:(invitations, forms, stationery, etc.)					$3,500.00	3.48%	
32								
33	Ad Journal:(print 80% of estimated total attendance)					$3,000.00	2.99%	
34								
35	Awards:					$400.00	0.40%	
36								
37	Decorations:					$1,000.00	1.00%	
38								
39	Miscellaneous:					$750.00	0.75%	
40				Sub-Total		$34,090.00	33.92%	
41	In-Kind Offset:					$5,000.00		
42								
43	TOTAL EXPENSE:					$39,090.00	38.90%	
44								
45	NET REVENUE:					$61,410.00	61.10%	
46								

remaining revenue categories. The per-seat reservation price is an "estimate" and depends on an agency's natural constituency; the size, locale, and economic base of the community; the type of event the organization is producing; and what sister nonprofits are charging. The agency's executive and event committees must consider all of these factors. It is also calculated by making a "rough" estimate of the event's basic costs: meals, site rental, special circumstances—for example, a combination sports tournament and dinner event—as well as any out-of-the-ordinary costs for invitations, speakers and their travel expenses, and special award costs. These are some of few items that can raise basic costs. (They will be discussed in detail in Chapter 7.)

Exhibit 3.2 shows what a typical pricing pattern would be for a testimonial event. An advertising journal is assumed for this event so that the packaging concept could be illustrated; later in the chapter there is a discussion on packaging which will further clarify this subject. Obviously, if the testimonial is part of an athletic tournament such as a golf tournament, then revenue can be obtained from sponsorships of each Tee, and a silent auction of various golf equipment, etc. Every different type of event has its special sponsorship possibilities, and it's up to the nonprofit's professional staff and lay leadership to be creative and originate the revenue source.

CALCULATING REVENUE SOURCES

Revenue sources are different for different events. A gala award dinner featuring dancing and entertainment, and where the main sources of revenue are derived from reservations and advertising in the program book, has different funding sources from a less-formal dinner with an auction, where revenue can be obtained from multiple sources. Whether revenue or expense, research into the minutiae of the line-item

Exhibit 3.2   Tribute Event Pricing: An Example

Individual reservations:	$150 each
Gold table of ten:	$1,500 plus $1,000 for gold-page ad
Silver table of ten:	$1,500 plus $500 for silver-page ad
Gold-page ad	$1,500
Silver-page ad	$750
Black-and-white full-page ad	$500
Black-and-white half-page ad	$250
Black-and-white "Good Wishes"	$150

entry must be the guiding beacon. Revenue is more difficult to calculate since the first line item depends on attendance, and that depends on many factors. Later in this chapter, the technique of estimating attendance is described. It is an exercise that can be used to clarify the mystery of revenue estimates.

Calculating the revenue starts with completing the Estimating Attendance Chart, Exhibit 3.3, which forecasts the minimum income the event can expect to generate from seat reservations. The event should be planned around a revenue mix with individual reservations (minimum-priced reservations) making up approximately two-thirds of the total revenue. Always keep in mind what the seven goals have as their ultimate aim: people. Bring people together so they can see for themselves the work of the nonprofit in their community. Achieve the goals, and support will surely follow! The remaining one-third of the revenue comes from the other sources of income: donations, in-kind gifts, sponsors and underwriters, program advertisements, and the packaging of these items into attractive marketing units.

ESTIMATING ATTENDANCE: CALCULATING MINIMUM REVENUE

A nonprofit's aim in producing a special event is to realize the seven goals, which will result in maximum attendance at the event. Exhibit 3.3, Estimating Attendance, is a method by which an agency can calculate how to achieve goal 1: raise money. It combines a planned networking process (described in detail in Chapter 5) that anticipates the *recruitment* of the event chairs selected by the agency's governing board, who *categorize* these people according to where they believe the candidate fits into the community's social hierarchy. The result of this exercise is an approximate base attendance figure that will allow the event committee to construct a minimum revenue figure. This information will allow committee members to do their job: to reach a total budget revenue figure based on this minimum figure, calculated with a degree of logic, so they can sell enough additional ticket reservations (and solicit other revenue described in this chapter) to fill the event site to its capacity.

Estimating how many people will contribute to the event can be an insurmountable task for an agency that has never produced a special event; it can involve guesswork even for an agency that holds one every few years. To take the unknown out of the attendance equation and to take the guesswork out of the budget line item, rows 6, 9, and 10 are the result of completing Exhibit 3.3 and 3.3a (CH0303.DOC and CH0303a.XLS).

Exhibit 3.3   Estimating Attendance

One of the most important tasks of special event leadership is to choose event chairs who can motivate guests to support an event. Classifying them in this manner will provide a "base" to relate to the revenue section, reservation budget line (rows 6, 9, and 10 of Exhibit 3.1) when estimating revenue. This chart should be used in conjunction with Exhibit 3.3a, the Input Sheet for Estimating Attendance.

	Prominent Very active professionally and in community	*Well-Known Occasionally active in the community*	*In-House Active only with the agency (2 premium tables total)**
Event Chairperson	5–10% (and 1 premium tables)*	4–8%	3–5%
Honoree	5–8% (and 1 premium tables)*	3–5%	3%
Event Co-Chairs	3–7%	2–4%	3%
Committee Members	Committee members are expected to purchase at least one ticket to the event.		

*Note: Premium Tables of ten are sold (at premium prices above the "base" ticket cost) for their prime location and usually in conjunction with an ad in the program journal. (This is referred to as packaging.)

    Apply above percentages to "benchmark" attendance figure: Divide *desired* dollar goal by a ticket price per seat that is attainable in your community; see example below.

    Estimated attendance = Total Gross Revenue of $100,000 is required to achieve net income of approximately $70,000. Approximately two-thirds of gross revenue equals desired net income.

    Use the gross revenue amount—$100,000 divided by $150 (attainable community ticket price)—to obtain a reference figure of 667* potential guests. The reference figure will now be referred to as the "benchmark" figure.

    This following matrix applies the percentages from the chart applied to benchmark figures to complete calculations:

	Prominent	*Well-Known*	*In-House*
Event Chair	33 to 67 guests	27 to 53 guests	20 to 33 guests
Honoree	33 to 53 guests	20 to 33 guests	20 guests
Event Co-Chairs	20 to 47 guests	13 to 27 guests	20 guests
70 Committee Members	The "benchmark" figure of 667 guests is rounded to 70. Ten percent of the "benchmark" figure is an *ideal minimum* number of committee members.		

Note: Nonhonoree (award/tribute dinner) events require recruitment of more committee members.

* $100,000 ÷ $150 = 666.666. This chart rounds up to 667. Exhibit 3.3a does *not* round up the resultant figure.

Exhibit 3.3a Input Sheet for Estimating Attendance

	A	B	C	D	E	F	G	H	I	J
1										
2										
3	To obtain Bookmark Figure (Cell C 6) Insert Amounts in Cells C 4 and F 4									
4	Estimated Gross Revenue:		$100,000.00		Per seat price	$150.00				
5										
6	Bookmark Calculation Figure:		666							
7										
8										
9										
10			Prominent		Well-Known		In-House			
11										
12	Chair	Low%: 5% =	33	4% =	26	3% =	19			
13		High%: 10% =	66	8% =	53	5% =	33			
14	Honoree	Low%: 5% =	33	3% =	19					
15		High%: 8% =	53	5% =	33	3% =	19			
16	Co-Chair	Low%: 3% =	19	2% =	13					
17		High%:7% =	46	4% =	26	3% =	19			
18	Committee Members: This category is responsible for 10% of the benchmark figure:						67			
19		TOTAL LOW % =	85		58		19			
20		TOTAL HIGH % =	165		112		71			
21										
22										
23										
24										
25										
26										
27										
28										
29										
30										
31										
32										
33										
34										
35										
36										
37										
38										
39										
40										
41										
42										

At this point, be aware that all formulas that rely on the effort of committees—professional and volunteer—are just that, formulas. They are only methods based on years of experience producing special events that were successful because everything worked—the honoree was credible and had not been indited by the grand jury the week before the event; the event chairs were interested enough in the work of the agency to put that extra hour of effort into making the event a success; and the pricing of the event was within reason for the community (and, oh yes, the planets were in perfect alignment).

Special Event Attendance Factors

1. Size and community prominence of the nonprofit's board of directors
2. Number of current donors
3. Size of the current prospect list (names on the computer database who have not made a gift for the past two fiscal years, or never made one)
4. Drawing potential of the nonprofit's natural constituency (a subjective factor)
5. Uniqueness of the event in the community (also a subjective factor)
6. Size and prominence of the special event committee—what Exhibit 3.3, Estimating Attendance, is all about

First to be considered is the nonprofit's status in its community. In addition to the prominence of its members, the size and makeup of the board indicates the organization's links to every ethnic, political, cultural, social, professional, and business group in the community. A good example is the new public library in San Francisco. The fund-raising committee of the board of directors organized their capital campaign as described in this book: They organized every neighborhood in the city. They put together a huge committee whose tentacles reached every group and community in the city. It was a classic marketing plan, and the results went beyond everyone's dreams. The organization received gifts from people who had never before given to a nonprofit capital campaign.

The current donors are the prime candidates to invite to the event and to ask to volunteer on the various event committees. A list of more than 500 of these donors provides a support base to work with; fewer than that will require the event committee to make an extra effort to recruit event volunteers and to network for nonaffiliated supporters. (See Chapter 5 for specific ideas.)

The number of and up-to-date information on past or lapsed donors (those who have not made a contribution for the past two years) is critical information for the potential success of the special event. These people once thought that the nonprofit was worthy of their support, so now is the time to go back to them with a few concrete proposals: Ask them to volunteer for the special event or, if that is not possible, to purchase a table or seats, and/or an ad in the program journal.

The identification of and the drawing potential of an organization's natural constituency is vital for a successful special event. For example, schools must keep their alumni lists up to date; churches, mosques, and synagogues must appeal to their members and to the greater circle of their religious affiliates (social services and health and human relations agencies) and to other nonmembers of the sect who have worked with the congregation. Remember, the religious leader is also a community leader, and so it is perfectly acceptable to invite to the event community leaders and organizations he or she has worked with over the years; in fact, members of those organizations would be insulted if they were not asked to participate.

In large metropolitan communities, it is vital that the event be creative and unique. These locales represent large potential audiences who are sometimes overwhelmed with invitations to special events. To catch their attention, the event must be innovative. Even in a nonmetropolitan, more isolated community, it is a good idea to look deeply into the inner workings of the area, to talk to people and ask for their ideas. Often something that has always been around and seems to be part of the woodwork can provide a unique situation for a special event.

The final factor concerning special event attendance has already been discussed in detail: the number and prominence of the special event committee, a key factor in producing a successful special event. There are never enough committee members. They alone guarantee a base of attendance at the event and are the first line of contact with an agency's natural constituency and community. (See Chapter 4 for an in-depth discussion on the recruitment of committee members.)

WORKING WITH EXHIBIT 3.3: ESTIMATING ATTENDANCE

This exhibit is part one of a three part exhibit series: Exhibit 3.2, Tribute Event Pricing, Exhibit 3.3, Estimating Attendance, Exhibit 3.3a, Input Sheet for Estimating Attendance, and Exhibit 3.5, An Actual Attendance Matrix.

Exhibit 3.3a is an automated version, where numbers can be imputed in cell 'C4' Estimated Gross Revenue and cell 'F4' Per seat price and they will automatically calculate the bookmark figure, cell 'C6,' and will translate all of the percentages shown from rows 10 to 20 to actual high and low attendance numbers of Exhibit 3.3, (on Excel) and can be downloaded from the disk that comes with this book.

Exhibit 3.3 is the intuitive engine that provides the information for Exhibit 3.6 and ultimately, Exhibit 3.1, the sample budget. The first matrix of Exhibit 3.3 shows the percentages that can be assigned to the special event volunteers: Event Chairperson, co-chairs, and committee members (committee members are not assigned a percentage, they are only expected to buy one ticket; this is a conservative approach. On a practical level, committee members usually purchase two seats, and sometimes more.) It also has a category for an honoree at a testimonial dinner.

The categories: Prominent, Well-Known, and In-House are descriptions that define volunteers that you will endeavor to recruit for the special event.

The percentages refer to the number of guests that these volunteers will try to sell tickets to for the event. Percentages have been conservatively calculated and are based on many years of experience in producing special events. These percentages are applied to the benchmark figure which is explained in detail in the second section of Exhibit 3.3, and is obtained from Exhibit 3.2, Tribute Event Pricing. In the third section of the exhibit the result of the percentage calculations multiplied by the benchmark figure, low and high values, are shown for each category.

The results of Exhibit 3.3 are then outlined in Exhibit 3.5, An Actual Attendance Matrix.

How do the percentages get assigned, e.g., when should the high one be used? In the Introduction we discussed the Seven Goals for a Successful Special Event. Goal number three is Motivation. Motivation leads to enthusiasm. Now, we discuss the "big ifs": if your chair, co-chairs, and committee members are excited about the event; continually coming up with ideas on other corporate, business, and professional people to approach for ticket sales, donations, advertisements, etc., and the majority are in the Prominent or Well-Known categories, consider using a higher percentage. The staff professional will know when this is happening; the energy level and the requests for information from the volunteers will be obvious. If it is absolutely overflowing with enthusiastic energy, then use the higher percentage figure; if there are any reservations, then increase the low percentage by one or two points. An experienced development professional will intuitively know what is happening with "his/her" event committee.

Exhibit 3.3 illustrates nine categories where percentages are to be applied to a number that will be used to calculate estimated attendance. Seven of these categories indicate a percentage range; for example, if an event has a prominent chairperson, a range of 5 to 10 percent should be applied to the benchmark number used for calculation purposes.

Now comes the tactical part of "strategy and tactics"; tactics are the people part of special events. Which comes first, tactics or strategy? They both do! They are initiated simultaneously. But, when pencil is put to paper, usually planning occurs first and organization, second. In other words, the type of special event a nonprofit is going to produce will have been discussed for some time since including an event in the development plan was first suggested. The following expressions state the case succinctly:

PLANNING = STRATEGY = TYPE OF SPECIAL EVENT

ORGANIZATION = TACTICS = PEOPLE

BUDGET = STRATEGY + TACTICS

Exhibit 3.3 includes a category for each of the chairperson(s), co-chairs, and committee members, all of the people who are involved in the special event. (See Exhibit 4.1 for a listing of the duties and responsibilities of everyone involved in a special event.) The honoree is special because not all events have one; if an event does, the event is classified as a testimonial award or tribute event; the term "honoree" is interchangeable with "celebrity" in a golf tournament, movie preview, or an auction where a well-known person is involved. When producing its first event, an agency must have a way to make a *conservative* attendance estimate. Exhibit 3.3 provides this method.

Use Exhibit 3.3 as the master exhibit, followed by, in sequence, 3.2, 3.1, and 3.5, to get a full picture of what estimating attendance is all about. Remember, estimating is an inexact process and is very subjective.

Defining the Categories in Exhibit 3.3

A *prominent* person is interpreted in the corporate world as the chairperson or chief executive officer of one of the largest utilities, financial institutions, or retail, service, or industrial businesses in the area who is also active in the community and associated with local charities. Similarly, professional leaders, attorneys, physicians, accountants, and religious leaders also can be classified as prominent.

Well-known people come from the same social and community scene as prominent people, but for their own reasons, keep a somewhat lower profile. They might be managing partners of a law firm or an accounting office or an executive or senior vice president in the corporate world.

In-house leaders are an agency's own volunteer supporters who have been active on the executive or development committee. They are usually the most conscientious and most productive workers, but often are not known in the general community, though they frequently are well known in their own constituencies—church, fraternal, professional, and neighborhood groups. Agencies that overlook these people do so at their own peril!

These categories might seem to be a "snobbish" way to define lay leaders, but, in fact, many volunteers look at the hierarchy of nonprofit agencies in this way. Prominent and well-known people have the resources, connections, and energy to motivate other people. In-house lay leaders are the "worker bees," who are known for their dedication to the nonprofit.

WHAT ITEMS MAKE UP GROSS REVENUE

Gross revenue is the total of all the money collected for a specific fund-raising program. As applied to special events, it is the sum of:

1. Guest seat reservations
2. Revenue from advertisements in the ad journal (also known as the event program)
3. Packaging, which combines the sale of complete tables plus an ad in the program journal
4. Donations people mail in in response to the event invitation
5. Corporate or individual underwriter of the entire expense of the event
6. Sponsorship(s) from businesses or individuals that support a particular segment of the event
7. In-kind donations (these are offset in expenses, but they should be included to show a true picture of the income and outgo of funds for the event)

The main purpose of a special event is to attract as many people as possible. While the remaining sources of income will bring in money, the sources are not tied directly to bringing more people to the event but to increasing revenue. Concentrate on selling premium tables, which accomplishes two tasks at one time: It brings in additional guests and leads to advertisements in the program journal (not to mention additional income). Next, focus on ad/program journal income; follow that by securing in-kind gifts and donations.

PACKAGING OF PREMIUM TABLES
AND ADVERTISEMENTS

Most special events offer premium "gold" and "silver" tables, packaged with an ad/program journal for added revenue. Marketing regular tables (10 × $150) can be enhanced by offering a discount package of a full-page black-and-white ad and a table of ten for $1,800 instead of the separate price of $2,000. If organizations and individuals are going to spend $1,500 for a table of their own, an additional $300 for a full-page promotion is a bargain. The budget example indicates that the committee can calculate gross ad journal income at a rate of 10 percent; donations from invitees who cannot attend are calculated at 3 percent; and in-kind gifts at 5 percent of gross revenue. These estimates are conservative and are subject to local conditions; when in doubt, lower them.

UNDERWRITERS AND SPONSORS

Underwriters and sponsors provide a source of income so special they cannot be included in a sample budget, because only some nonprofits have access to this funding source for their special events. In special event fund-raising terms, an underwriter is not a *guarantor* (the usual meaning of the term). When a corporation or individual underwrites a special event, it picks up the entire cost of the program. For example, BigHeart Development Corporation will pay all of the costs for our sample testimonial event: dinner, wine, site rental, printing and postage, awards, decorations, and miscellaneous expenses. The quid pro quo is identification. BigHeart's name is on every piece of stationery, mentioned in every press release, and shown on advertisements, and it is prominently written about in the ad journal. This pure concept of underwriting is rare.

Usually underwriting is accomplished by one corporation or individual in conjunction with others. The hybrid result is a "main" underwriter that partners with other organizations that are known as "sponsors." The main underwriter pays for the largest amount of expense; the others (sponsors) pay for smaller items, such as the wine, flowers, awards, and printing and postage.

How does a nonprofit find the "right" underwriter and sponsor? Are there steps an agency can take to plan a strategy to obtain underwriting and sponsors? The answers to these questions are: yes and yes!

Identifying a potential underwriter/sponsor is step 1. To do so, draw up a list of corporations that are actively marketing their goods or services in the community. Utilities, banks, telephone companies, savings and loans, insurance companies, and home-grown businesses that maintain headquarters in the community are all potential underwriters. Divide the list into the following categories: national/international corporations, regional businesses, and local companies. Now draw up a list of the segments of the special event that can be underwritten and match the prospective underwriters with these segments. This constitutes the strategic plan and is graphically displayed in Exhibit 3.4 (CH0304.DOC). Once the potential underwriters are identified, the exhibit will show what segments are logical for a particular underwriter to fund. Remember, though, that who funds what is an arbitrary decision; on a practical level, depending on the amount required, any of the underwriter designations could provide funding for any area.

Implementing tactics is the next step. In the nonprofit world, the lay leadership and volunteers implement tactics. Chapter 4 shows how to organize the event committee, the group of chairpersons and committee members who have the ties to the corporations and businesses in the community. Prepare a dossier on each prospective underwriter and what segment the event executive committee thinks it can fund; then solicit people from the committee to make an appointment between the proper corporate executive, the lay leader, and a member of the nonprofit's professional staff. Take the case statement (see Chapter 4) that has been assembled from the worksheets and the agency's marketing material to this meeting.

Exhibit 3.4   Underwriters and Sponsors Matrix

Special Event Funding Opportunities ⇓	International and National Corporations	Regional Businesses	Local Companies Headquartered in the Community
Catering			
Preevent Receptions			
Printing Formal Invitations			
Program Book (or Ad Journal)			
Wine			
Table Favors			
Advertising (Media; TV; Radio)			
Printing Miscellaneous Documents			
Postage			
Honoree Awards			
Entertainment			
Guest Speaker Expenses			

IN-KIND DONATIONS

The agency is sponsoring a golf tournament; a lay leader involved with the event approaches a major golf equipment manufacturer and solicits a gift of all the golf balls needed for the tournament with the agency's logo on one side and the manufacturers name or logo on the other. The expense section of the event budget saves a lot of money, the manufacturer receives a great marketing coup with your prestigious group (and at a net cost to them that cannot be imagined); everyone is happy. The same thing can be accomplished with wine, beer, bottled water, printing, special desserts, and a host of items that can make the event's ambiance just that much better and in the process lowers the overall cost and increases the net revenue.

Why is this shown in the budget? Technically, it doesn't have to be, but to show an accurate fiscal accounting of the event why hide it? There is no reason to do so. But, make sure that what is added into revenue is also added to the expense section of the budget.

REVENUE CONSIDERATIONS FOR EVENTS IN SMALLER COMMUNITIES

Smaller scale and practicality are the key words when an event is produced in a small community that lacks a large population and an industrial infrastructure, not to mention a superstar. Yet even smaller events can attract underwriters and sponsors. For example, a small nonprofit with a tiny list of supporters and no corporate sponsors can produce an event at the local community center or a potluck breakfast, lunch, or dinner (provided by the nonprofit's volunteers, "the underwriters"). An ad journal program can be produced on the computer (charge $25 per ad), plus a per-seat charge of $10 to $20, may draw 50 to 100 people, with minimal expense. In between the plain-vanilla and superstar event lies a vast number of options for a nonprofit. Remember, all of the tools described in this book will work with any nonprofit, large or small. Many times it is more fun to be a big fish in a small pond. Refer back to the Introduction for the discussion on creativity and the local community.

MASTERING REVENUE AND EXPENSE ITEMS

Expenses are easier to figure than revenues because estimates are as near as the telephone. Vendors want an agency's business and so will provide quotes quickly. However, fine-tuning the expense figure requires research. For example: How many people can you conservatively expect to attend an event? How many invitations were mailed (a major factor that incorporates printing, postage, list maintenance, volunteers, and/or mailing house labor)? (See Chapter 7.) These are just a few items that need researching. A full list is provided and discussed later in the chapter.

The expense amounts in Exhibit 3.1 are not actual dollar figures. Prices for meals and site rentals and other expenses vary widely around the United States, as they are subject to the laws of supply and demand. Revenues also vary according to the constituency the agency is trying to attract. Nonprofits in smaller communities usually charge somewhat less than what the same event would command in, say, Los Angeles or New York. Pricing an event is an art, not a science. To achieve all seven goals, nonprofits need to attract as many people as possible. If an event is unique, be aware of the "greed" factor: Avoid trying to squeeze the last dollar from potential attendees. This can result in very few attendees! Be fair and follow the nonprofit golden rule: Do not charge others what you would not pay or charge for a reservation.

Revenue: Behind the Line Items

We'll begin at row 6, individual reservations. This line item shows the results of the Estimating Attendance Exhibit 3.3, which has already been explained in detail in this chapter. Although referred to as "individual" reservations, they are actually reservations sold to the community at $150 per guest; this line also includes complete table reservations (tables seat ten people) at the basic price of $150 per guest, or $1,500 per table.

Rows 9 and 10 reflect the premium tables sold as a package—that is, program advertisement of one gold or silver page and a table of ten for $2,500 or $2,000 per table. These are sold *only* as complete tables. Although usually sold to corporations, partnerships, and so on, they can be sold to a group of individuals who are closely connected to the nonprofit or to the honoree. Instead of receiving one check, then, the nonprofit receives a number of checks from each purchasing unit.

Location of these tables near the "action"—the table of honor or head table—is in many cases more important than the advertisement the purchaser takes in the ad journal. This is why both gold and silver ads are offered. The gold package table is located closer to the table of honor and/or head table than the silver and the black-and-white packages. The details of putting together the ad journal and packaging the advertisements can be somewhat Machiavellian. Assuming that all special events have an honoree, celebrity, or some other incentive, such as an early tee-off time at the golf tournament, that makes it a desirable place to be on that particular date, a scenario of bidding for the best packages the nonprofit can offer can be constructed.

Because the possibilities for the premium line items are limited only by the imagination of the event committee, the exhibit indicates only the basic premium categories in the revenue and expense budget. When the main attraction at an event is both a person deserving the agency's award and a celebrity (movie or stage star or sports hero), then everyone will want to meet this person, have dinner with him or her, and show their closeness by purchasing the largest, most prestigious package offered: a platinum-page advertisement located on the back cover or inside back or front covers, a table of ten located near the table of honor, and admission to the preevent reception. It is easy to add this premium line item to the budget—but do not do it in the euphoria of the moment when the budget is planned. Make doubly sure that these premiums can be sold to the agency's natural constituency or community.

Next, we look at row 12, donations. Initially, it may seem too good to be true! People are responding to initial invitations by mailing in checks with a note saying that they will be out of town and cannot attend the event. The event committee, board of directors, and executive director all proclaim: "Let's have a nonevent. It's pure profit! No dinners to purchase, no extra expense. We'll make a killing." At this point, someone has to remind them that raising funds is only the first goal of a special event. There are six other goals that the agency wants to achieve and a special event is the best way to accomplish them. That is why it was chosen in the first place. Many nonprofits use donations to subsidize longtime supporters who cannot afford the $150-per-seat reservation, only the $45 cost of the meal. Donations subsidize the remaining $105. A deserving volunteer will work three times as hard for a nonprofit if treated like the "big" kids. Remember, this subsidy process must be accomplished with understanding and tact.

Row 14 addresses ad journal revenue. By definition, only three premium ad journal goodies can be offered: the program's back page and inside front and back covers. The remaining ad journal revenue is derived from gold, silver, and black-and-white full-page, half-page, and "good wishes" advertisements. Ad sales can be an important source of revenue. If possible, put together the largest committee of sales types that are available—it will pay off.

Row 16 is for in-kind gifts, which are great, if they are useful items such as wine, bottled water, cellular telephones, table favors, printing, good-quality advertising specialties (pens, etc.), coffee, and tea, just to mention a few. If the community is located in a unique area, such as Hawaii, in-kind gifts such as special leis for the honoree and event chairs and regular leis for the attendees are very welcome. In-kind gifts sometimes create problems: For example, a volunteer who is a business owner of a retail store and who has a large quantity of an item in stock that did not sell as planned may think, "What better way to move this item than to donate it to a charity!" However, there was a reason the item did not move: It was shabbily made, badly designed, or not in good taste. Do not touch it. The event will be judged by what is provided for the guests. If they receive something that is not in good taste, the original donor will never be known, but the agency will be remembered as one with little class and taste.

Expenses: Behind the Line Items

Expenses vary so widely from one area to another that it would be foolish to provide concrete examples. The percentages shown in the budget example are just that: examples. They are guidelines; planners will have to survey costs in the local area to plug in actual amounts. In-kind gifts are offset in the expense side of the budget so that a true cash budget can be presented to the board and the event committee.

Expenses are semifixed because basic costs are usually unchangeable. The post office will not give a discount on a 32-cent stamp (see discussion on nonprofit postage rates in Chapter 7) so, unless an organization obtains an in-kind donation or a corporate sponsor who will underwrite specific items, expenses are here to stay. Some suppliers will give nonprofits a lower price or trade an item for an ad in the program. This bartering is very good practice for the nonprofit, because the cost of an advertisement in the program is minimal compared to a retail item like bottled water or wine, even when corkage charges that the hotel, country club, or caterer will charge are taken into account.

Row 23 is for food. The $45 price is based on the standard three-course meal: salad, entrée, and dessert, with coffee, tea, or milk. Most nonprofits speak to the catering manager at the hotel or facility where they are going to hold the event and have him or her suggest a menu. There is a better way! Exhibit 7.1 in Chapter 7 details the menu and service an agency wants to provide. Use this exhibit as a bidding form. It is especially handy when dealing with off-site caterers.

Row 25 is for beverages. At dinners, it is customary to serve wine. For breakfasts and brunches, coffee, tea, and milk are the beverages of choice. At lunches during the work week, wine is sometimes served, but not as often. In general, $14 will buy a decent 750-ml bottle of wine.

Row 27 is the corkage expense, which applies only if the nonprofit provides the beverage and the caterer has to handle it—that is, open a wine bottle (hence the designation).

Tip: This expense item is usually the most negotiable when discussing the event meal price with the catering manager. (See Chapter 7.)

Row 29 is postage. Although there is a nonprofit postage rate, invitations should be mailed first class. That said, if expenses are climbing at an astronomical rate, this item can be lowered. (See Chapter 7 for detailed information.)

Rows 31 and 33 cover printing. Again, draw up a detailed specification to submit to three or four printers, in order to receive the lowest bids. If possible, recruit someone from the printing or design community to serve on the event committee. (See Chapter 7 for a detailed discussion and suggestions on this very important subject.)

Rows 35, 37, and 39 deal with awards, decorations, and the famous *miscellaneous item* line. Depending on how formal and glitzy an event is going to be, these items are almost interchangeable. If decorations are the committee's passion, then spend money on them and give a paper award—a parchment document—suitably framed in plain black molding. Event chairs can choose people to be in charge of these areas, but someone must make sure that they do not go wild and overspend.

Row 41 is for in-kind offset. This is an accounting balance line. Since the agency did not cut a check and pay for the in-kind donations, double-entry accounting still has to account for the gift. Hence, what goes into the revenue is taken off after all expenses are totaled.

PUTTING IT ALL TOGETHER

The 667 "benchmark" attendance figure is used as an example to fill in the following matrix using percentages from Exhibit 3.3, Estimating Attendance. The following assumptions are used: The event chair is classified "prominent"; the honoree and co-chair #1 are "well-known"; co-chairs #2 and 3 are "in-house"; co-chair #4 is "prominent"; for simplicity and to be conservative, committee members are not placed in a category; as described in Chapter 4, when the event committee members accept the invitation to be part of the event, they do so knowing that they are agreeing to purchase at least one seat reservation. Even a lazy, uninterested event committee will produce a minimum of at least their own number in reservations. So, 70 committee members can be expected to sell between 70 and 140 seat reservations. (Some of those will be for their significant others.)

The example of the actual matrix, Exhibit 3.5 (CH0305.DOC), indicates a range of 230 to 325 potential guests; conservatively, use the 230 guest reservation figure to project *part* of the reservation income shown in line 6 of the budget in Exhibit 3.1. That budget line indicates 450 seat reservations at $150 per seat for a total income of $67,500. Where does that figure come from? It's a big jump from the conservative estimate of 230 seat reservations at $150, 20 reservations at Gold Tables for $5,000, and 10 Silver Table seats at $200. There is a potential shortfall of 220 reservations. Each of the 70 event committee members have been counted on for only one reservation. (The chart does not assign a percentage figure to the event committee members.) The real

Exhibit 3.5 An Actual Attendance Matrix
(Percentages from Exhibit 3.3 have been rounded up or down to the nearest tenth or fifth.)

Leadership	Prominent	Well-Known	In-House	Event Committee Members	Gold Table 10 guests/ table	Silver Table 10 guests/ table	Estimated Revenue
Event Chair	35–70				2 tables @ $2,500 each	1 table @ $2,000	$12,250 to $17,500
Honoree		20–35					$3,000 to $5,250
Co-Chair 1		15–30					$2,250 to $4,500
Co-Chair 2			20				$3,000
Co-Chair 3			20				$3,000
Co-Chair 4	20–50						$3,000 to $7,500
Committee Members	Calculate 70 reservations from committee members						$10,500
Total Reservations	55–120	35–65	40	70	20	10	$37,000 to $51,250 230 to 325 Reservations

value of these committee members is their outreach to the larger community and to their own natural constituency. In discussions, the nonprofit professional and the event chair must stress the importance of each committee member bringing his or her significant other plus another couple to this event. Doing so is very easy for committee members, especially if it is explained clearly at the event committee meeting. (See Chapter 5.) That will account for 210 additional reservations. When the number is this close, another ten reservations is not difficult to find. The event leaders signed on because they know the standing of the honoree and the reputation of the nonprofit will benefit the community. They want the event to be a success and will work very hard to make it so.

But there are no guarantees in life or in special events fund raising. That is why the recruitment of event leadership is so crucial to the success of the event. The budget is an important piece of the plan that will ensure the recruitment of the most energetic and prominent lay leaders in the community.

The matrix shows two figures for some categories and only one for the others; this is in accordance with the percentages shown in Exhibit 3.3. The lower one, which estimates 34 percent of the attendees (55 + 35 + 40 + 20 + 10 + 70 = 230 divided by 667 potential guests [the "benchmark" figure]) and 37 percent ($37,000) of the event revenue. Selling the remaining seat reservations at $150 to raise the additional $69,600, ($150.00 × 457 potential guests) for total revenue of $100,550 is the object of this exercise. Building an expanding core of enthusiastic supporters will ensure the survival of an agency during the periodic valleys of economic unrest and downturn. However, to be realistic, a nonprofit agency cannot rely solely on selling an additional 457 seat reservations. Although it is tempting to budget using the potential full attendance, do not succumb to this temptation. Conversely, the leadership should not build a budget understating the potential of the event. Having arrived at this point in planning a special event and with the full support of the board and main monetary supporters, some degree of optimism can be built into the budget.

The volunteer lay leaders are *not* expected to purchase all of these reservations from their own pockets. Their businesses, the names they provide of people they will personally contact (see Chapter 5), and reservations they make using their own funds will account for the extra seat sales.

Calculation of gross revenue is an art, but applying a methodology to it by using the Estimating Attendance worksheet (Exhibit 3.3) provides a step up: the educated guess!

COMPUTER SPREADSHEETS AND DATABASES: HOW THESE TOOLS CAN HELP YOU KEEP THE EVENT AND THE BUDGET ON TRACK

When responses come in from mailings and invitations, some will include checks and some will just indicate that the person or organization wants to reserve a table, seat, or advertisement. A computer database program designed with the correct fields, such as those in Exhibits 3.6, 3.7, and 3.8 (▪CH0306.DOC, CH0307.DOC), can store, sort, and print out this data in various reports that will make informing the chair and co-chairs an easy chore. There are two routes to take: Purchase a proprietary program and install and run it on a computer, or use the database program already on the computer with the fields outlined below to produce a basic database and reports. There are many database programs to choose from; for advice, ask someone at a sister nonprofit about the database used there or contact an organization that assists nonprofits for a recommendation and assistance. The disk included with this book contains Exhibits 3.1, 3.2, and a sample of a plain-vanilla but useful database. All have been presented in spreadsheet form, even the database, on Excel 97.

Exhibit 3.6 Database Fields Required for a Basic Special Event Report

Field Description	Field Name	Field Length
First Name	FNAME	
Last Name	LNAME	
Day Telephone	DAYPHONE	
Organization	ORG	
Guest Reservation(s)	GURES	
Running Total—GURES	RTGURES	
Per-Seat Price	SPRICE	
Running Total—SPRICE	RTSPRICE	
Advertisements	ADVERT	
Running Total—ADVERT	RTADVERT	
Donations	DONATE	
Running Total—DONATE	RTDONATE	
Paid	PAID	
Running Total—PAID	RTPAID	
Date Reservation Received	DATE	
Comments		

If an agency puts on a major special event every year, a reception once or twice a year, and other miscellaneous events and meetings, consider investing in a special event computer program. A new program on the market, developed by Certain Software, Inc., is Event Planner Plus, which is described as an all-in-one event-planning application. It can easily save a nonprofit time and money by gathering all your vendor information, plus the prospect list, event budget, and seating arrangements and many other reports in one place. It is easy to learn how to use and functional.

Exhibit 3.7   Revenue and Expense Budget Line Descriptions

Revenue	Expense
Individual Guest Reservations (including special categories)	Meals
Full Table Reservations (including special packages)	Site rental
Donations	Catering (for sites without in-house kitchens)
Program Journals	Beverage cost
Underwriting	Corkage (for donated beverages)
Sponsors	Postage
In-kind contributions	Printing
	Awards
	Decorations (flowers, table favors/ balloons, etc.)
	Photography
	Miscellaneous
	In-kind gift offset
	Entertainment
	Marketing (public relations and advertisements)
	Insurance
	Security
	Video presentations

CONCLUSION

This chapter explained how the budget links together planning and organization, which are implicit tools in the seven goals. Using Exhibit 3.2
and 3.3 as a guide, the planning committee can develop a reliable Revenue and Expense Budget (Exhibit 3.1), which is used to plan networking
for recruitment of co-chairs and community committee members.

The budget also dovetails with the tasks outlined in the METT. The
timetable details every task associated with revenue and expense line
items. Every week can be printed separately and the tasks associated
with the period can be assigned to the appropriate staff member or volunteer lay leader. The results provide a to-do system that can be accomplished easily in small steps. The following example from the METT
outlines week number 1:

Exhibit 3.8 Sample Revenue and Expense Report
(See Exhibit 3.6 for field descriptions.)

	A	B	C	D	E	F	G	H	I	J	K	L	N
1	LNAME	FNAME	GURES	RTGURES	SPRICE	RTSPRICE	ADVERT	RTADVERT	DONATE	RTDONATE	RTPAID	COMMENTS	
2	Armstrong	Jim	5	5	$750.00	$750.00					$750.00	Meat only	
3	Cooley	Martha	2	7	$300.00	$1,050.00					$1,050.00	Veggie only	
4	Wendroff	Alan	10	17	$1,500.00	$2,550.00	$500.00	$500.00			$3,050.00	Near Honoree	
5	Wiley	John & Sons	10	27	$1,500.00	$4,050.00	$1,000.00	$1,500.00			$5,550.00	Sponsor	
6	NSFRE/GGC			27		$4,050.00		$1,500.00	$1,000.00	$1,000.00	$6,550.00		
7	Gore	Al	10	37	1500	$5,550.00	1000	$2,500.00	$500.00	$1,500.00	$9,550.00		
8											$9,550.00		
9													
10													
11													
12													
13													
14													

METT Checklist for Chapter 3

Week	To Do This Week	Ref.	☑
1	Draft revenue and expense budget:		
	a. Set pricing for the event.		
	b. Research expense items to estimate costs.		
	c. Determine the amount and variety of in-kind gifts that need to be solicited.		
	d. Plan strategy for underwriting and sponsorship funding.		

CHAPTER FOUR

Recruiting Volunteer Leadership for Your Event

"All real living is meeting." (Martin Buber, I and Thou*)*

FIRST ENLIST THE STAKEHOLDERS

Stakeholders, as the name implies, are those people who have an interest beyond just giving money and attending the free cheese-and-cracker receptions. Stakeholders sit on the board of directors, executive committees, and working program committees and include people who give big bucks and are available at any time for advice sessions. These are the folks to talk to before embarking on the journey to put on a special event. Make the case with these people, then proceed with the assurance that with a plan and their contacts, there is an excellent chance to achieve success and an opportunity to do something great for the agency. Without their support: Forget it!

Look for the most prominent people in the community. Such people are always on the go and involved in many projects, both for profit and nonprofit. Many times they affiliate with socially visible organizations, such as the symphony, opera, and ballet in metropolitan areas, and in smaller communities, the annual pageants, whether it is the Fourth of July celebration or the Christmas tree lighting festival.

Questions frequently asked by nonprofit boards include: What is our role in the special event structure? How do we recruit the event chairs and committee members? What are their duties? and Why do non–board members assume these responsibilities? To recruit board members successfully, nonprofit staff should have the answers to these questions ready in advance. Once the agency board and staff professional have read the first four chapters of this book, they will be ready to begin recruiting the event chair(s) and co-chairs. It is important that these leaders sign on board the event committee almost immediately after the nonprofit's governing board has agreed to producing the special event. "Urgent" is the best way to describe the recruitment process. Why? Because without this leadership nothing can go forward: An event date cannot be scheduled and a site for the event cannot be chosen. To recruit the best leadership, people should be chosen on the basis that they will be involved with making key decisions involving the event. All of the documents required to accomplish this important job are described in detail in the following pages. Exhibits 4.1 through 4.4 can be thought of as the recruitment papers.

Please follow closely the systematic organization and filtering process outlined, it will assist in obtaining a head start in the recruitment of your key leadership. Later in this chapter the case statement will be described and the exhibits mentioned will come into play. Prepare this information in advance to facilitate recruitment of the chairs and the community-wide committee members for the event. Exhibit 4.1 (▓CH0401.DOC) is the event organization chart.

AGENCY GOVERNING BOARD

The Agency Governing Board (sometimes known as the Executive Committee) consists of the key stakeholders and are seen at the top of Exhibit 4.1. They hold the overall responsibility of managing the non-profit and establish policy guidelines and monetary goals for every facet of the fund-raising program, including the special event. They appoint the members of the agency's development committee, set a fund-raising example for the entire board of directors by making a yearly leadership gift, and assist the professional staff to solicit the board gifts. Usually they are the resource for introductions (network-ing) to potential chairpersons, and also they provide names of people the committee can invite to join the larger community-wide committee. Obtain this information by interviewing each member of the governing board and the board of directors.

AGENCY DEVELOPMENT COMMITTEE

The Agency Development Committee appointed by the governing board, is composed of people who actually are responsible for planning the event. They choose the type of event that would best suit their agency based on the nonprofit's financial needs and overall develop-ment plan. A special event is one segment of the agency's development program; since it encompasses the natural constituency and/or the entire community, it must fit the nonprofit's "personality." For example, a health agency would feel comfortable sponsoring a community 10K walk and run, which would be completely out of place for a more seden-tary human and social services nonprofit such as a university research institution. The agency development committee appoints the chairper-son for each of the agency's programs, including the special event. The development chairs are charged with monitoring every fund-raising program as to its goal and the amount of funds raised and how they are collected. One of their most important jobs is motivating board mem-bers and volunteers. Motivation takes the form of encouraging these people to make a gift, to ask others to make a gift, and to work with the professional staff in a program of donor (current and potential) stew-ardship. A unique feature of special events is the opportunity it gives

Exhibit 4.1   Event Organization Chart for a Special Event: Duties and Responsibilities

---

AGENCY GOVERNING BOARD
(Sets overall policy and fund-raising goal)
  a.   Appoints members of development committee.
  b.   Sets leadership example with their financial commitment.
⇓

AGENCY DEVELOPMENT COMMITTEE
  a.   Plans overall fund-raising activities for the fiscal year.
  b.   Appoints chairs for each fund-raising program.
  c.   Monitors fund-raising goals on a scheduled basis.
  d.   Motivates board members and volunteers.
⇓

1.   EVENT CHAIRPERSON   ⇔   AGENCY PROFESSIONAL
  a.   In charge of overall planning, strategy, tactics, and implementation.
  b.   Recruits required co-chairs and dinner committee members.
  c.   Is agency's public representative for the event.
  d.   Coordinates all event activities and supports all co-chairs when required.
  e.   Contacts and recruits all honorary chairperson(s).
⇓

2. EVENT CO-CHAIR	3. EVENT CO-CHAIR
⇓	⇓
(in charge of dinner event committee)	(in charge of marketing/public relations)
a. Prepares invitation letter package.	a. Works with event chair and other co-chairs to make sure all constituencies are contacted.
b. Builds list of potential members.	
c. Prepares meeting agenda.	
d. Follows up with committee members re: solicitation efforts.	b. Prepares press releases.
	c. Is liaison with all news media.
	d. Contacts all needed in-kind donors.

4. EVENT CO-CHAIR	5. EVENT CO-CHAIR
⇓	⇓
(ad journal chair)	(hotel and catering)
a. Plans pricing for journal.	a. Coordinates with agency professional on selection of event site.
b. Designs solicitation letter.	
c. Builds mailing list of prospects.	
d. Works with agency professional to design "event packages", i.e., ticket sales plus journal ads.	b. Assists with selection of menu.
	c. Helps agency professional in negotiating food service contract.

6.   HONORARY CHAIRPERSON(S)
⇓
(past honorees, community leaders, politicians)
  a.   Recruited by event chair.
  b.   Politicians arrange for certificates of honor.
  c.   Community leaders assist in obtaining news media cooperation.
  d.   Past honorees assist in renewing support of their organizations.

7.   COMMUNITY-WIDE EVENT COMMITTEE MEMBERS
⇓
(community representatives)
  a.   Attend one and only committee meeting.
  b.   Agree to support event individually and/or organizationally.
  c.   Agree to mail at least ten letters to potential guests.

shy and reluctant people to start the solicitation process at a relatively small "ask"; when that experience is successful, they almost always feel more self-assured and are ready to be trained to solicit larger amounts.

This committee appoints the actual special event chairpersons as well as the chairs for the other fund-raising programs. The interlinked worksheets, labeled Exhibits 4.2, 4.3, and 4.4 (CH0402.DOC, CH0403.DOC, CH0404.DOC), form a set of filters, starting with a large list of potential names and ending with the recruited special event chairpersons. These are the tools for a process that is referred to as reverse networking.

REVERSE NETWORKING

The usual networking process involves asking everyone for names and then finding a lay leader who can make the introduction to the specific person. Reverse networking refines the selection process by choosing from Exhibit 4.2, the Community Leadership Assessment, names of those people whom committee members feel would be the most effective chairs; generally they are the most prominent leaders in the community. Although this might be construed as elitist, it is a practical method that will give an event a better chance of being successful. Many times no one on the committee knows prominent people, and members throw up their hands in frustration; do not let this happen. With more discussion a committee member may suddenly remember that a friend does know the person in question. With that lead, the recruitment process begins. Exhibit 4.3, Leadership Recruitment, is the first filter. Section A lists five spaces for recruitment of the event chairperson. (Five potential candidates are usually enough.) Section B is for the co-chairs; a typical event requires four to six, as outlined in Exhibit 4.1. In both sections place the number-1 candidate in the first slot; list the other names according to the committee's best-qualified determination. It is prudent to set up a contact schedule with assignments for each network contact person: Carpe diem (seize the day) is the watchword. The event cannot proceed until these recruitments are completed.

Exhibit 4.4 is the form to use when a position has been filled. Sometimes, two or more chairs or co-chairs are recruited, in that case list them on Exhibit 4.4, horizontally rather than vertically, and alphabetize by the last name from left to right.

Special note

When interviewing the number-1 candidate for event chair, show him or her the documents that are a part of the Special Event Case Statement, Exhibit 4.7. *Make sure* that only that person's name is listed as the

Exhibit 4.2   Community Leadership Assessment

List Community Leaders from the Corporate, Political, and Professional World		
NAME	AFFILIATION	AGENCY CONNECTION

Exhibit 4.3   Leadership Recruitment

A.   Candidates for Event Chairperson (only 1 is required)
(Choose from governing board, volunteers, or professional/corporate contributors)
Please note: List more prospects than you require. Once a volunteer has accepted, others can be asked to take another leadership role or to serve on the community-wide committee.

	Name	*Affiliation*	*Network Contact*	*Comments*
1.				
2.				
3.				
4.				
5.				

B.   Candidates for Event Co-Chairpersons (4 to 6 required)
(Recruit from recommendations given by event chairperson, those who were general chair candidates, and community volunteers who are current contributors.)

	Name	*Affiliation*	*Network Contact*	*Comments*
1.				
2.				
3.				
4.				
5.				
6.				
7.				
8.				
9.				
10.				
11.				
12.				

number-1 candidate and that no other names are shown. Do not give this person any indication that he or she is anything but the one and only choice.

THE EVENT CHAIR AND AGENCY PROFESSIONAL

The professional and the event chair now take charge of the day-to-day planning and organization of the special event. The strategy and tactics outlined thus far are now refined and implementation begins. Most of

Exhibit 4.4   Leadership Posts
"Who's on First"

(Use in conjunction with Exhibits 4.1, 4.2, and 4.3 for leadership recruitment)

The following people have accepted these positions:
1. Event Chairperson(s)
      a. _____
      b. _____
2. Co-chair—Ad Journal
      a. _____
3. Co-chair—Site and catering
      a. _____
4. Co-chair—Community-wide event committee
      a. _____
5. Co-chair—Marketing and public relations
      a. _____

the work is accomplished by the agency professional, based on discussions and sign-off by the event chair.

The event chair will now have to choose their co-chairs. He or she have some suggestions as to the best choices on the committee's list; the chair might have some people in mind that the committee has not thought about. This involvement by the event chairperson should be encouraged. He or she is putting someone's name before the public and, as such, endorsing the agency and the event, so the chair should have a strong say in who he or she wants to work with. In the co-chair comments section of Exhibit 4.1, indicate which co-chair position a person might feel comfortable with because of profession or interest.

Another important task for the event chair is the recruitment of the honorary chairpersons. If the chair is classified as prominent, recruitment will be fairly easy. If the chair is not in the public eye, then the event committee and the agency development committee together should determine how these honorary chairpersons are to be contacted and what they should be asked to do.

CO-CHAIR RESPONSIBILITIES

The co-chair responsible for the *community-wide event committee* assists the professional in building a potential committee membership list using resources obtained from the honoree, the event chair, and the agency's own existing list of current, lapsed, and potential donors. The co-chair signs off on the invitation letter; usually the event chair does so as well. (See Exhibit 4.5.) The co-chair prepares the committee meeting agenda and is the main contact for the committee members throughout the weeks preceding the event. (Chapter 5 describes duties of the event committee.) The community-wide event committee co-chair and the event chair are very active in the beginning of the community-wide recruitment drive; the more members who sign on, the better ratio of success the agency will receive for the event. For example, by estimating an attendance of 500 guests at the event, a 100-member community-wide committee will ensure at least 150 paying attendees, or 30 percent of your estimate, weeks prior to the event. The old saying, "the more the merrier," is very applicable for a special event community-wide committee.

Exhibit 4.5   Assignment of Responsibilities: Dinner à la Heart

1. Chairperson of Associates
   a. Member of GIOA board
2. Chairperson, Dinner à la Heart
   a. Makes all final decisions for Dinner à la Heart
   b. In charge of all committees; recruits committee chairpersons
   c. Establishes event timetable
   d. Updates Dinner à la Heart information sheet/brochure
3. Restaurant committee chairperson
   a. Makes list of restaurants to solicit
   b. Up dates contract, menu, and information forms
   c. Assigns restaurants to solicit to committee members
   d. Working with event chair, sets pricing for each restaurant
   e. Works with event chair on reservations, seating, and resolves conflicts that arise
4. Chairperson for corporate underwriting and major gifts
   a. Prepares list of prospective corporations to solicit for underwriting and sponsorships
   b. Prepares price schedule and acknowledgement benefits for underwriters and sponsors
   c. Determines what in-kind gifts are needed and prepares list of potential donors to solicit
5. Host & Hostess chairperson
   a. Appoints co-chairs for the following:
      1. Overall invitation list committee
      2. Restaurant amenities, e.g., centerpieces and table decorations and IOA marketing materials
      3. Identifies board or staff member to act as host/hostess at each restaurant
6. Marketing chairperson (because of their experience, professional staff is very involved with this committee)
   a. In charge of all printed material, developing the advertising schedule, and the design and distribution of these items:
      1. Save the date cards
      2. Formal invitations
      3. Contracts and menu forms
      4. Restaurant and corporate solicitation letters
7. Press releases and media, radio, and television contacts
8. General letters to restaurants and after the event "thank-you" letters

The event co-chair responsible for the *program or advertising journal* (referred to as the ad journal) is next in line in responsibility for generating revenue for an event. This job is tailor made for volunteers with experience in professional advertising agencies or public relations. They have experience dealing with graphic designers, printers and mailing houses, and, of course, the public. The ad journal, if priced and designed correctly, can be packaged with table sales; it can become the "tail that wags the event." The co-chair uses the lists generated by the event chair for invitations plus building a special corporation and business mailing list. The agency professional assists the co-chair with the logistics of preparing the special ad journal solicitation kit and cover letter; the chair and co-chairs, with input from the nonprofit's professional, determine the pricing of the packages. Chapter 5 examines the details for this important revenue and programmatic publication in detail.

The co-chair in charge of *marketing and public relations* is next in line regarding timing and importance. If there is a large corporate presence on the committee, try to enlist an in-house marketing or advertising department executive for this post. This co-chair will work with the other co-chairs as well as the agency's programmatic staff. He or she will make sure that all constituencies served by the agency are contacted—that they receive an invitation to serve on the event committee or at least to attend the event. Unless the agency's professional staff has had experience or special training in working with the press or writing press releases, this co-chair will be the main contact with the fourth estate. (Chapter 6 gives details and sample documents.) This co-chair frequently takes on the task of contacting suppliers for in-kind gifts, such as wine, soft (and sometimes, hard) drinks, table favors (such as a pen with the agency's logo), and cookies or candy. Depending on the membership of the event committee, this co-chair makes sure that all goods and service providers who are members are given an opportunity to bid on the needs of the event. Often these vendors will offer wholesale prices, donate items and services, or barter a specialized item for an advertisement in the ad journal. A more detailed description of these creative activities is found in Chapter 6.

The co-chair in charge of the *site and catering* should be someone who has acknowledged taste concerning food and decor and can select an appetizing menu. He or she must be knowledgeable about the special dietary considerations of the constituency. This person should be able to work with the caterer or hotel catering department and come up with a menu that is reasonable in price and also represents the area's specialties. For example, on either coast of this country fresh fish is usually in abundance during many months of the year; if an event is held in such an area, do not import exotic fish entrées from Hawaii when it is possible to serve excellent salmon caught that morning. When negotiating with the hotel catering department or an independent caterer, remember that labor is a big part of their costs. While the choice of poultry, meat, or seafood can alter the price of each meal, that cost is small in relation to the waitpersons' salaries. The success of the event can depend on an adequate number of well-trained waitpersons. The most successful hotels and caterers do well because they give honest prices for their events. Also, they understand the constraints nonprofits have concerning costs, and they usually will give a nonprofit a break on corkage (the price charged when the agency supplies its own wine or liquor). A good example is the practice followed in San Francisco. Many events use wine donated by winemakers from the nearby Napa Valley; if a hotel ordinarily charges $14 to $25 per bottle but charges only a $5 to $8 corkage fee per bottle, the savings are significant. Similar savings can be obtained if the dessert is donated.

WHO'S ON FIRST?

A good method to use to remember strategies and techniques is to give them a familiar name. Borrowing the title from Abbott and Costello's classic baseball story, *Who's on First*, the organization chart of the major players and their responsibilities for Dinner à la Heart, our example from the Introduction, is an excellent way to follow how an event is produced. Please go to Exhibit 4.1 on page 84 and look at the Organization and Responsibility chart. This chart can be modified for any special event. Its main purpose is to construct a frame around the event that the volunteers can use to attach their responsibilities. When planning many special events the budget projections would be made before the recruitment of lay leaders. Dinner à la Heart is different because the expense and revenue items, although similar to other special events, are a factor of obtaining "the product": the restaurants. Signing up the restaurants determines the budget figures and to sign up the restaurants—volunteers are needed. When the budget is constructed the restaurant's pricing policies will also be outlined. Also, events like this are usually produced by an established volunteer group, in this case they call themselves: *The Goldman Institute on Aging Associates (GIOA).* Since recruitment is not usually a crucial factor, the assignment of responsibilities and constructing a budget can take place simultaneously. The main jobs are outlined in Exhibit 4.5.

THE COMMUNITY-WIDE EVENT COMMITTEE

Members of the community-wide event committee are the ones who toil in the trenches. They are the up-front marketing and public relations volunteers. They should represent every constituency in the community. By signing on, they have agreed to the following:

- Attend the one and only committee meeting
- Support the event either through their organization or individually
- Send a certain number of letters to potential guests (and follow up by telephone)

Their job description and responsibilities are defined in detail in Chapter 5.

HONORARY CHAIRPERSONS

Federal, state, and local politicians together with prominent community leaders who support a nonprofit or want to be associated with it for prestigious reasons make excellent honorary chairs. If the event is an annual testimonial type, do not forget to invite past honorees to serve as honorary chairs. Doing so will indicate to the public the continuity and standing of an agency with local decision makers. Very often, past honorees are excellent choices to serve as an event chair. The more prominent the past honoree is, the better the opportunity an agency has to attract the news media to write about the event prior to the actual date. Of course, any media coverage is welcome, but it helps if this is before the event: It can help sell tickets.

Politicians are natural candidates for honorary chairs; what better way to seek endorsement for them than to be associated with a nonprofit that is doing so much good in the community? Remember, however, that everyone associated with an event is not necessarily of the same political persuasion. Always ask elected politicians from all political parties represented in the community. Choose politicians carefully. Lately it seems that many politicians are being investigated for ethical and other problems. The event chair and his or her committee will usually know what is going on, and an agency professional must rely on their advice (and consent).

Should honorary chairs be asked to pay for their dinner, lunch, or green fees? Yes! Politicians have campaign funds for this purpose; prominent community leaders are either wealthy enough or will have their organizations pay the bill. There are always exceptions, however; check with event leaders if there is any doubt about the honorary chair's ability to pay the ticket price.

The success of special events depends on the ability of the volunteers. Their motivation is critical to the outcome of the event. Motivation techniques do not have to be sophisticated; communication is one of the best motivators for a special event.

The agency's support staff who are assigned to work on the special event are the key people in this process. They inform the event chair (or designed co-chair) of all communications received from the mailings to the prospective event committee members, all revenue received, ad journal advertisements, and in-kind contributions. The support staff is also guided by the METT, and any deviations they experience must be communicated to the professional and event chair. After the formal invitations are mailed, the chairs and the event committee members must be informed on a weekly basis of the current number of reservations received and the other items that will appear on the event log. This log is set up on the support staff's computer. (See Chapter 3 for details.) In order to make this mailing to the chairs easy, the number of mailings are calculated in advance. Every time a chair or committee member is recruited, a batch of envelopes is made for the member. When the event log is to be mailed, usually on Friday afternoon, copies are made and mailed to all the appropriate volunteers. This alone is an excellent motivation piece, but, when it is followed up with a telephone call from the event chair and/or co-chairs and sometimes the agency professional, pointing out the progress made to date and what remains to be accomplished, it stirs committee members to make the contacts that they have let fall by the wayside. Another motivation technique is to enclose with the event log any newspaper articles about the agency's program work in the community or internal information about a new community program. This information is very helpful to committee members when they talk to prospective guests. Another technique that committee members can use is to print up on business card stock all of the pertinent information about the event for the members to give to people they meet during the day. (This can be accomplished on the agency's computer at a very modest cost.) Samples of this card and other documents are presented in Chapter 6.

VOLUNTEERS AND COMMUNICATION

The quote at the beginning of the chapter, "All real living is meeting," is particularly apt when an agency works with volunteers. Meeting is not only being introduced to someone, it is also a means of communi-

Exhibit 4.6   Volunteer Checklist

Volunteer Name and Telephone No.	Reporting Station	Report To	Time Period	Duties	Dress Code	Confirmed with Volunteer
Betty Bright	Reception Desk	Fran Do-Good Coordinator	6:00–7:00 P.M.	Greet VIPs	Cocktail Dress	Yes: 5/28/98
Rich Reliable	Check in desk	Event consultant	5:30–6:30 P.M.	Check-in guests/ table assignments	Business Attire	No: as of today

cation. Special events, to be successful, have to be equal; in other words, everyone must be a part of the process. Special events are complex programs. In order to succeed, they usually involve volunteers. Consider this example. Recently, events that could have led to disaster occurred at what turned out to be a successful event. A prominent nonprofit gave a gourmet dinner, featuring four different chefs cooking and baking their specialties; the event was preceded by a reception and a silent auction. The event was held in the lobby of a large office building, which was given over entirely to the nonprofit for the evening. A prominent restaurant occupied one corner of the lobby; its chef had agreed to let his colleagues from the other restaurants work in his kitchen that evening. As one can imagine, the food was spectacular.

The volunteers were asked to arrive at a certain time and enter by a specific door. When they arrived, the door was locked and a hastily lettered sign directed them to another entrance (with a very vague arrow that pointed into the air). Upon finally obtaining entrance, they were directed to an area for assignment (no prescreening or instruction given) and told briefly what they were to do. Fortunately, the volunteers were experienced and fast learners.

After the event, some volunteers asked the nonprofit's volunteer coordinator what had happened. The answer: The event planner/consultant had not included the coordinator in the plans for the event. To prevent the waste of this most valuable resource, organizations should use a checklist like the one in Exhibit 4.6 (CH0406.DOC).

A CASE STATEMENT FOR SPECIAL EVENTS

Special events require a case statement, as do capital and annual campaigns, but for completely different reasons. The overall success of a special event depends largely on the achievement of the seven goals. To

Exhibit 4.7   Special Event Case Statement Planning Document

1. An up-to-date mission statement (See the Goldman Institute On Aging mission statement in the resource section.)
2. The Seven Goals statement
3. Planning statement for the event taken from Exhibit 2.1, which determines the special goals for the event.
4. Agency's program brochures and planning documents
5. Special event committee organization chart, Exhibit 4.1, along with a filled out Leadership Posts, Exhibit 4.4 (if possible)
6. Master event timetable—from week 1 to the conclusion of the event
7. Proposed event budget, Exhibit 3.1
8. Details on how attendance was estimated, Exhibit 3.3, with the input sheet
9. Sample committee invitation letter and inserts required for the event, Exhibits 5.1 and 5.2
10. Agendas for the chair and general committee meetings, Exhibit 5.4
11. Event committee information kit documents for the one and only event committee meeting, Exhibit 5.3
12. Sample of a proposed time line and script for the actual event, Exhibits 9.1 and 9.2

make sure that they are achieved, the budgeted attendance must be attracted. The event committee's job is accomplishing that task. Recruitment of event chairs and co-chairs is crucial to achieving that objective. A case statement will help with this recruitment. Therefore, it is the key ingredient in producing successful events.

To establish a nonprofit's case and help recruit the desired people to be leaders and committee members, prepare a binder containing the special event's main planning documents. Examples of these documents are available on the floppy disk that comes with this book. Briefly, they include the items listed in Exhibit 4.7.

When meeting with a proposed event chair make sure that the lay leader is fully briefed on the documents described in Exhibit 4.7. Plan the interview as a major gift solicitation would be planned.

METT Checklist for Chapter 4

Weeks 1 thru 9	To Do This Week	Book Ref.	☑
1 a)	Recruitment planning begins in week 1		
2 a)	Board members are recruited for event positions		
b)	The reverse networking process is started		
c)	Community-wide recruitment begins		
d)	The case statement for your event is assembled		

CONCLUSION

Recruitment of the volunteers—chair(s), co-chair(s), and event committee members is the key to a successful special event. These volunteers should understand the scope and reasons for putting on the event; as the seven goals teach us, there is more to a special event than raising money.

The process of recruitment is explained and outlined, with exhibits that assist the reader at every step. Starting at the beginning, with the stakeholders, those people who are already volunteering, e.g., the board members, major contributors, and the existing volunteer base. Representatives from the stakeholder group, either through the development committee, or an ad hoc committee assembled just for this event, assist the professional in finding the first one or two chairs, who, by using the exhibits provided in the chapter, start recruiting the other volunteers.

Finally, a recruitment tool, the Case Statement for Special Events, is introduced.

CHAPTER FIVE

Networking in the Community

THE COMMUNITY-WIDE EVENT COMMITTEE— THE MARKETING TEAM

In Chapter 4, the event leadership was recruited. Now the members of the community-wide committee must be identified and signed on. These are the people who will become the agency's marketing team. They will relate its story to their friends and colleagues and, in the process, encourage them to support the event. In reality, they accomplish both public relations and marketing: By telling the agency's story, they are marketing the event; by soliciting support for the event, they also become the public relations team.

Networking is a chain reaction somewhat like the play *Six Degrees of Separation,* which is based on the assumption that no person on earth is more than six contacts away from every other person. Networking is one of the most important skills a special event committee member must learn and practice. For example, the agency's leaders recruit the event chair, who in turn recruits the co-chairs; they in turn recruit the honorary chairs and event committee members, who fan out into the community and solicit support for the special event.

Possible Event Committee Candidates

The first list of potential members is obtained from the event leadership. Once the event chair and co-chairs have agreed to become involved, they usually provide a list of friends, professional colleagues, and vendors. Business names can be obtained from the newspaper's business section and various business publications published in the area. In many metropolitan areas a business publication called the *Business Times* is published weekly. Every year this weekly publishes a gold mine for special event fund raisers; *The Book of Lists.* Each list gives information on the top 25 organizations in each business category, and there are some 50-plus categories, ranging from accounting firms to women-owned businesses. If this type of business paper is available, take a look at it. It can give an agency a step up in locating prospects to become potential supporters.

The agency's list of current and past supporters, suppliers (accounts payable), and corps of volunteers also should be included on this master list. Unless the agency, and the event, is designed for very limited appeal, everyone is to be invited, because, unfortunately, everyone will not respond to the invitation. There is no exact ratio between expected attendance and the number of people wanted on this committee; a guiding principal is: The more the merrier! (See Chapter 3's Estimated Attendance Chart, Exhibit 3.3, for a conservative approach to this question.) Is it cost effective to mail 1,000 first-class committee invitations for a possible 5 to 10 percent return? The answer is yes. If only 50 people respond positively and agree to serve on the committee, then at least 60 to 75 people will attend the event; the mail will probably deliver 20 to 30 donations from those who cannot serve because they will be out of town on event day. Those people who did not respond will receive a formal invitation from the agency's office or a committee member; one of the objects of networking is to make it possible for people to receive at least three notifications of the event four to eight weeks prior to the event date.

Exhibit 5.1 (CH0501.DOC) is a generic committee invitation letter; such letters should be kept to one page using this paragraph sequence: introduction naming the event and, if applicable, the honoree, and the date and location of the event (recipients who get this far might read the remainder); the "why" of the event; an outline of the nonprofit's programs; then the "hard sell," asking readers to join the committee and what is expected of members; a highlighted, centered paragraph giving the day, date, time, specific room, and location of the one and only committee meeting; a reminder on how to join by returning the enclosed card; and most important, a thank you.

Exhibit 5.2 is the sample return card that is enclosed with the committee invitation letter. The number of return cards the agency office receives is the first clue to whether the event will be a smashing success, average, or a potential failure. Return cards that come back with more checkmarks in boxes 1 or 2 of side A (the person will join the committee, box 1 indicates the person can attend the meeting; box 2 indicates the person cannot attend) are positive indications. If box 3 on side A is checked, all is not lost; some people just do not relate to committees, and they still might make a reservation and attend the event. However, if the last seven words of that sentence are crossed out (and this happens) then forget this person: "... ~~count on me to support the event.~~" Make sure the event chair(s) look at these particular return cards. They might know the respondent and can find out if the person has had past problems with the agency or just does not participate in special events.

Side B of the card shows possible preevent reservations and indications of advertisement sales.

To summarize, the potential event committee member receives Exhibits 5.1 and 5.2 and a return envelope (which need not be prestamped).

A Few Housekeeping Items

The next step in the event committee process is preparing the documents for the one and only committee meeting. Before that takes place there are some chores to complete:

Exhibit 5.1   Committee Invitation Letter: An Example

January 1, 1995

James S. Armstrong, CFRE
Director of Development
St. Vincent de Paul Society
5616 Geary Blvd. Suite 207
San Francisco, CA 94121

Dear Jim,

I have the pleasure of serving as one of the Chairpersons for the Frank Brennan Award Dinner. The 1995 tribute will honor Stephanie Brown, Ph.D., and Roselyne C. Swig. This prestigious event will be held in the Gold Room of the Fairmont Hotel on Wednesday, March 29th.

The St. Vincent de Paul Society is honoring Dr. Brown and Roselyne Swig for their outstanding leadership and support of those in need in our community.

The Society will also present the Ozanam Medal to Marilyn Christen and Dr. Michael Sander on March 29.

Nineteen ninety-five celebrates one hundred and fifty years of Vincentian service in the United States to those who need a helping hand. The St. Vincent de Paul Society works in every level of our community to break the cycles of homelessness, substance abuse and battering.

We would be honored to have you serve with us on the Dinner Committee. As a member of the committee, we ask that you support the dinner by either purchasing a table or helping to put a table together. In addition, a souvenir journal is being prepared for our honorees. Your involvement will help insure a successful event. The *only* committee meeting will be held on:

Thursday, February 9, 1995
5:30 to 6:30 p.m. Squire Room on Lobby Level
Fairmont Hotel, San Francisco

Please complete and return the enclosed card indicating your support of this event and confirmation of your attendance at the Dinner Committee meeting.

Thank you in advance for your participation and support, and on behalf of my co-chairs, I look forward to seeing you at the Dinner Committee meeting.

Sincerely,

_____

Used with permission from St. Vincent de Paul Society, San Francisco.

Exhibit 5.2   Sample Return Card for Event Committee Invitation Letter

★★ ## ST. VINCENT de PAUL SOCIETY BRENNAN AWARDS DINNER

★★ *Thank you for inviting me to serve on the Dinner Committee for the Frank Brennan Awards*
★★ *honoring Stephanie Brown, Ph.D., and Roselyne C. Swig on March 29, 1995.*

★★ ☐ *I am happy to serve on the Dinner Committee and will attend the only committee meeting*
★★ *on Thursday, February 9th, at 5:30 p.m., in the Squire Room at the Fairmont Hotel.*

★★ ☐ *I will be pleased to serve on the Dinner Committee but am unable to attend the committee*
★★ *meeting on February 9th. Please send me all materials necessary for me to support the event.*

★★ ☐ *I am unable to serve on the dinner committee, but please count on my support*
★★ *for the event.*

★★ Name _____

★★ Address _____

★★ City _____ State _____ Zip _____

★★ Phone _____ Fax _____

Side A

★★ ## ST. VINCENT de PAUL SOCIETY BRENNAN AWARDS DINNER

★★ *Please reserve the following for the Frank Brennan Awards Dinner honoring*
★★ *Stephanie Brown, Ph.D., and Roselyne C. Swig on March 29, 1995:*

★★ *DINNER & ADVERTISING PACKAGES*
★★ ☐ *Platinum Underwriter ~ $5,000. Table of ten ~ priority seating and Gold Page ad in Dinner Journal.*
★★ ☐ *Gold Patron ~ $2,500. Table of ten ~ and Gold Page ad in the Dinner Journal.*
★★ ☐ *Silver Patron ~ $2,000. Table of ten ~ and Silver Page ad in the Dinner Journal.*
★★ ☐ *Bronze Patron ~ $1,500. Table of ten ~ and Full-Page ad in the Dinner Journal.*
★★ *Please telephone (415) 379-7814 for information on covers, centerfold, and presenting sponsorship.*

★★ *DINNER ONLY*
★★ ☐ *Please reserve _____ table(s) of ten at $1,000. per table.*
★★ ☐ *Please make _____ reservation(s) at $100. per person.*

★★ *SOUVENIR JOURNAL ADVERTISING ONLY*
★★ ☐ *Gold Page ~ $1500.*   ☐ *Full Page ~ $750.*   ☐ *Individual Listing ~ $200.*
★★ ☐ *Silver Page ~ $1000.*   ☐ *Half Page ~ $500.*   *Copy Deadline: March 17th*

_____   **Side B**

Used with permission from St. Vincent de Paul Society, San Francisco.

1. Set up a computer database of all responses from the event committee invitation letter; these can be sorted later, and the members' list can be printed directly from the database for the committee information list.

2. Sort responses to boxes 1 and 2 on Exhibit 5.2, side A, from the negative answer of box 3.

3. Create a committee list, describing all members' organizations, professions, and so on. (See Exhibit 5.4 for a sample committee list.)

4. Important note: Always look at both sides of the return card. Do not miss a reservation or advertising contract. Record these responses in your Reservation Log database. (See Exhibit 3.6.)

THE COMMITTEE INFORMATION KIT AND THE AGENDA FOR THE COMMITTEE MEETING

The invitation letter guaranteed potential committee members that there would only be one meeting of this committee, that it would last only one hour, and that all the information they required would be ready for them at the meeting. The committee kit is one of the motivational keys for the committee members; like the case statement, it shows off the agency's professionalism. Volunteers for nonprofit events like to be associated with organized events. The kit is assembled and placed in a two-pocket paper portfolio that can be obtained at any office supply store. Green is a good color for this folder. A name tag with the name and organizational identification of the committee member is placed on each portfolio. The documents outlined in Exhibit 5.3 go into this kit.

Exhibit 5.3 lists the pocket and order in which the documents should be placed. Most portfolios have dye-cut pockets into which a business card of the development director can be placed.

At the meeting, place the portfolios on a table at the entrance to the committee meeting room in alphabetical order. A staff member should be at this table to greet and welcome each member. Everyone, lay leaders and staff, must wear a name tag.

Exhibit 5.3   Committee Information Kit

Left Pocket	Right Pocket
Agency's mission statement	List of all committee members and their organizations (Exhibit 5.5)
Agency's current brochure	Ad journal contract
Current media articles	Sample invitation letter (Exhibit 5.6)
List of agency's board and executive committee	Suggestions on whom to invite to event (Exhibit 5.7)
Current agency newsletter	Invitation list form for submittal to agency (Exhibit 5.8)
List of past honorees (if event has a history)	Synopsis of guidelines for committee members (Exhibit 5.9)
Copy of "Save the Date" mailer and list of the committee members	Reservation cards for inclusion with committee member's letter (printed to fit #10 size envelope). (See Exhibit 5.2 for an example.) A pretyped card with the members name on it is also enclosed to be filled out at the meeting. (See Exhibit 5.4, the event chair's closing remarks.)

An event committee meeting serves many purposes:

- *Motivation:* All members meet each other and the event chairs. Members have an opportunity to talk to community leaders in a warm and relaxed atmosphere.
- *Information:* The event leadership team—chair and co-chairs— have the attention of the community event committee members and can explain how each member will contribute to the success of the event.
- The agency president and executive director expand on the mission statement so that the committee members can match the goals of that statement with the details of the agency's actual programs.

The actual agenda usually takes the form outlined in Exhibit 5.4.

Note: Many event chairs are hesitant to announce their commitment to the event; they do not like to boast. It is the duty of the executive or development director to point out to the chair that, on the contrary, the committee members would appreciate learning of the chair's support level because it gives them a guideline to follow.

Exhibits 5.5 through 5.9 are also part of the core documents for the event committee information kit. Exhibit 5.5 is the list of event committee members and their organizational affiliations; it is enclosed because committee members like to know who else is supporting the event. Exhibit 5.6 (CH0506.DOC) is the sample invitation letter event committee members are asked to send to their list of invitees; it follows a similar format used in the committee invitation letter (Exhibit 5.1). Potential attendees should receive the following communications about the event:

1. Save the date (mailed to the existing names on the agency's list during week 6). Names received after the event committee meeting also can be sent this notification, but usually the invitation letter (Exhibit 5.6) suffices.
2. Committee invitation letter (Exhibit 5.1)
3. Committee members personal invitation letter (Exhibit 5.6)
4. Ad journal letter and contract (sent to a select list)
5. Formal invitation

The object is to have every name on the list(s) receive at least three out of these five communications.

Exhibit 5.7 (CH0507.DOC) provides suggestions on whom committee member might invite to the event.

Exhibit 5.4   Committee Meeting Agenda

5:30–5:55 P.M.	Member check-in, greeting, and receipt of event information kit. Cocktails/soft drinks/fruit, cheese, and crackers are served until the meeting is called to order.
5:55–6:05 P.M.	Welcome by the event chair (who is usually the meeting emcee). a. Chair greets everyone and tells everyone about the honoree (if appropriate) or lays the groundwork for the event and why it is so special. b. Chair introduces the president and/or the executive director of the agency.
6:05–6:15 P.M.	Overview and description of the agency's work. a. Monetary goals of the event and how the funds will be put to use are discussed. b. Emcee introduces development director, who describes the work of the committee.
6:15–6:25 P.M.	Explanation of how the event committee can make this event a success. Development director a. Explains the guidelines and related documents, drawing special attention to the reservation card and the ad journal contract and how these items are packaged and the savings to the guests and businesses that will result. b. Explains the mechanics of list management and how important it is to mail, fax, or e-mail committee members' names promptly to the agency office. c. Answers questions.
6:25–6:30 P.M.	Close of meeting by event chair, who emphasizes the importance of each members' contribution to the success of the event. Chair now makes public his or her financial commitment to the event by telling how many tables he or she or his or her organization is purchasing and asking members to fill out the personalized reservation card enclosed with the kit (their names and organizations are already typed in) and make their commitment at this time.

Exhibit 5.8 (CH0508.DOC) is a simple list form for committee members to use to forward names to the agency for adding to the master mailing list and to make sure that the name is not a duplicate (either already on the master list or sent in by another committee member). (Sometimes it pays to send two mailings from two separate committee members; people who receive mailings from two prominent committee members become convinced of the event's importance).

Exhibit 5.9 (CH0509.DOC), Guidelines for Event Committee Members, summarizes the information the committee members receive from the development director during the committee meeting. The

Exhibit 5.5   Sample Committee List

Alpha Charity Tenth Annual Tribute Dinner
Honoring Ben Bigbucks
May 31, 1931

Senator Gloria Goodshoes   Representative Barb Barbar
Mayor Glen Green   Supervisor Jim Gladhand
Honorary Chairpersons

Henry Hanson   David Doright   Connie Contributor   Jim Jorquet

Dinner Chairpersons

Tribute Committee Members

Sam Sandlot
Athletic Shoes, Inc.

Jacob Corinson
Surveyor

Irwin Lindenbaum
Electrician

Peter Energy
Electric Utility Co.

George Greenbacks
Bank of the Wealthy

Jim Greenbeans
Coffee Beans are Us!

Dan Tastewell
Seashore Restaurant

P. Roland Gotsha
Public Relations

Shel Nebish
Super Computers

---

agency professional explains the following points, which are really
requests the event chair makes of the event committee members:

1. Put together a list of at least ten individuals, with their addresses,
    and telephone, fax, and e-mail, and either fax and/or mail it di-
    rectly to the agency to add to the master event list. The agency will

DATE
TITLE
COMPANY/ORGANIZATION
ADDRESS
CITY, STATE, ZIP

Dear Potential Supporter:

I have the pleasure of serving as a member of the Golden Gate Chapter's National Philanthropy Day luncheon committee. The luncheon will take place on Friday, November 15, 1996, in the Grand Ballroom of the Fairmont Hotel.

This year's tribute will honor James Hormel for Outstanding Philanthropist, Charlene Harvey for Outstanding Fund Raising Volunteer, Transamerica Corporation for Outstanding Corporate Grantmaker, and Jerry W. Mapp as Outstanding Fund Raising Executive. A Lifetime Achievement Award will be presented to Marjorie Stern and a Distinguished Service Award will be made, posthumously, to David and Lucile Packard.

Last year's Outstanding Philanthropist, Claude N. Rosenberg, will be our Honorary Chairman, for this, our Tenth annual awards luncheon.

The work of the Golden Gate Chapter of the National Society of Fund Raising Executives involves upholding the ethical standards of the fund raising profession and the education of lay leadership and professionals who are involved in philanthropic activities in the Bay Area. We believe that a dollar spent in training and education will produce a twentyfold return in support and economies to the nonprofit sector.

Your attendance at this event will ensure that our honorees receive the recognition they so richly deserve. I would appreciate your support of the luncheon by having your organization purchase an Awards Table, assisting us in putting a table together, or your individual support by purchasing one or two seats. I will be grateful for your support, and I know our honorees will also appreciate your involvement.

The luncheon will begin promptly at Noon and end at 1:45 p.m. in the Grand Ballroom of the Fairmont Hotel. Please contact me as soon as you have decided how many people from your organization will be attending (or, alternatively, how many people will be accompanying you to the luncheon).

Sincerely,

National Philanthropy Day Committee Member

NSFRE

National Society of Fund Raising Executives **Golden Gate Chapter** • 816 East Fourth Avenue, San Mateo, CA 94401 • Phone: 415-564-9300 Fax: 415-661-9708

Used with permission from Golden Gate Chapter/NSFRE.

Exhibit 5.7   Suggested Invitees

The Frank Brennan Award Dinner   **March 29, 1995**
Suggestions as to Whom to Invite   • Individuals on your accounts payable list.   • Other business leaders with whom you are friendly.   • People who have asked you for charitable contributions.   • Individuals with whom you serve on community committees and boards.   • Close personal friends (and relatives).   • Anyone you feel would want to honor Dr. Brown and Mrs. Swig and the Ozanam Medal recipients.

check for duplications and then contact the committee member with an okay to send the letter.

2. Using the sample letter (Exhibit 5.6) or the committee member's own variation, mail the letter with a reservation card (provided at the meeting and similar to side B of Exhibit 5.2) to each name on the list. Committee members are encouraged to insert a personal recollection of the event's honoree (if it is an award or testimonial event). Committee members are asked to use their own stationery (personal or business); if this is not possible, the agency should provide special stationery designed for the event. (Word processing programs can do this easily.)

3. If necessary, the nonprofit should volunteer to produce the letters for the committee members; usually retired and/or self-employed committee members appreciate this help.

4. The complete package includes the letter, reservation card, and a return envelope addressed to the committee member. It is easy for recipients to ignore requests from a "faceless" agency; ignoring a response addressed to the committee member at his or her office or home is more difficult.

5. Responses must be communicated immediately to the nonprofit agency's staff person, along of course, with the check.

6. Committee members should make a follow-up telephone call five to seven days after the letter is mailed. This is a gentle, low-key reminder call to encourage activity on the part of the recipient and to answer any questions.

The day after the committee meeting, mail the information kit to those committee members who could not attend the meeting. Include a short cover letter stating that one of the chairs or agency professionals will telephone to bring them up to date. (See Exhibit 5.10; CH0510.DOC)

Exhibit 5.8   Form for Committee Members to Record the Names of Their Invitees

COMMITTEE MEMBER _____ PHONE _____

Below is my personal list of individuals to whom I will send a letter for the dinner honoring

(PLEASE PRINT OR TYPE)

1. Name _____   Firm _____
   Title _____   Address _____
   Telephone _____   City, State, Zip _____

2. Name _____   Firm _____
   Title _____   Address _____
   Telephone _____   City, State, Zip _____

3. Name _____   Firm _____
   Title _____   Address _____
   Telephone _____   City, State, Zip _____

4. Name _____   Firm _____
   Title _____   Address _____
   Telephone _____   City, State, Zip _____

5. Name _____   Firm _____
   Title _____   Address _____
   Telephone _____   City, State, Zip _____

6. Name _____   Firm _____
   Title _____   Address _____
   Telephone _____   City, State, Zip _____

7. Name _____   Firm _____
   Title _____   Address _____
   Telephone _____   City, State, Zip _____

8. Name _____   Firm _____
   Title _____   Address _____
   Telephone _____   City, State, Zip _____

9. Name _____   Firm _____
   Title _____   Address _____
   Telephone _____   City, State, Zip _____

10. Name _____   Firm _____
    Title _____   Address _____
    Telephone _____   City, State, Zip _____

Exhibit 5.9   Guidelines for Committee Members: An Example

*NSFRE/GOLDEN GATE CHAPTER'S TENT
PHILANTHROPY DAY AWARDS*

*FRIDAY, NOVEMBER 15, GRAND BALLROOM—
FAIRMONT HOTEL—ATOP NOB HILL*

*GUIDELINES FOR NATIONAL PHILANTHROPY DAY
COMMITTEE MEMBERS*

1. Please write invitation letters to your personal list of friends and your organization's list of active volunteers. Please mail these letters *no later* than Friday, October 25, 1996.

2. Please send a copy of your list to our chapter office so that we can send formal invitations to these people.

    National Philanthropy Day Luncheon
    NSFRE/GGC
    816 East Fourth Avenue
    San Mateo, CA 94401

3. Please use your personal or organization's letterhead (or this one if you have access to neither). The sample letter we have enclosed should be modified with your personal comments concerning any or all of the honorees that you know.
4. Please follow up with a personal visit or telephone call about ten days after you have mailed the letter. This conversation should be a pleasant reminder of your interest in this event and your desire for their support.
5. Forward all responses to the chapter's office at the address above when you receive them. Please do not wait for everyone to respond before you send in the reservation; we need to know how many people are attending the luncheon as soon as possible!
6. Thank you for your assistance and support. It is appreciated. If you need more information or have any questions, please telephone: Alan Wendroff—415-285-4417; Wayne Strei—or the Golden Gate Chapter/NSFRE—415-564-9300; Facsimile: 415-661-9708.

N S F R E

National Society of Fund Raising Executives **Golden Gate Chapter** • 816 East Fourth Avenue, San Mateo, CA 94401 • Phone: 415-564-9300 Fax: 415-661-9708

Used with permission from Golden Gate Chapter/NSFRE.

Exhibit 5.10   **Letter to Committee Members that Miss the One and Only Meeting**

October 17, 1996

NAME
ORGANIZATION
ADDRESS
CITY, STATE, ZIP

Dear Colleague,

The tenth annual National Philanthropy Day Award luncheon is on its way to becoming a very successful event. As of this date we have almost 200 reservations.

As you know, I took over as the chair from Tom, due to a family emergency that requires most of his time in the coming months.

On Thursday, October 10, we held the one and only committee meeting to inform everyone who volunteered to help us what we needed to make this luncheon an overwhelming success.

As a member of our board, I am enclosing the information packet that was handed out that evening; by the time you receive this letter you should have also received the invitation to the luncheon.

Please take a few minutes to read the Guidelines in the enclosed information packet; if you need more information, please telephone me or Wayne Strei at 415-285-4417.

By the way, this year the luncheon will start promptly at Noon and end promptly at 1:45 p.m. All of us on the Host Committee guarantee this!

On behalf of all the members of the Host and Luncheon committees: Thank you for your help and assistance.

Sincerely,

Alan L. Wendroff, CFRE
Chairman, National Philanthropy Day Luncheon

N S F R E

National Society of Fund Raising Executives **Golden Gate Chapter** • 816 East Fourth Avenue, San Mateo, CA 94401 • Phone: 415-564-9300 Fax: 415-661-9708

Used with permission from Golden Gate Chapter/NSFRE.

UNDERWRITING THE EVENT: CORPORATE SPONSORSHIP

The event committee meeting is an excellent place and time to meet and talk to potential corporate supporters. Have a one-page bullet-point summary of the underwriting opportunities available. This summary can be part of the information kit, or the event chair can give it to the appropriate people. Arrange to have the event chair or a co-chair meet with interested executives at an early date. (See Exhibit 3.4 and Chapter 3 for an extensive discussion of underwriters and sponsors.)

LIST MANAGEMENT

Sometimes what we think are easy tasks turn into nightmares. List management is one of these tasks. We get hung up on getting peoples' names spelled correctly, on whether we have duplicate names in our database, and on what address should we use to send the letter or invitation. (This important task should be assigned to an agency support staff who has a working knowledge of the community and has a good eye for obvious misspelling of names. These people are hard to find; if the staff or the event chairs cannot find someone with this knowledge, a support staffer and a volunteer should work together on this.) People value their names sometimes more than their wealth. They will forever remember the agency in an unfavorable light if their name is misspelled.

It is no exaggeration to state the obvious: Lists of potential and current supporters are a nonprofit's lifeblood. Surprisingly, many agencies neglect to maintain these lists. Successful special events rely on up-to-date lists of names that are maintained on a regular basis; just like an automobile—that is, lists will wear out and the addresses and telephone numbers will get rusty if they are not lubricated.

When a nonprofit organization follows the guidelines outlined in this book to produce a special event, it will receive from the chairs and committee members a large influx of new names. The agency will also add names gleaned from various outside sources, such as local and business newspapers, the honoree's organization, religious institutions, alumni associations, and the Chamber of Commerce. Adding these names to the database of current, past, and potential supporters can cause the management information system manager to panic. Do the agency a favor and start a new database. It will probably not take up that much room on the hard drive. Names from the old database can be

METT Checklist for Chapter 5

Week	To Do This Week	Book Ref.	☑
5	Set date for event committee meeting.		
6 through 14	Event chair(s) continue to recruit committee members. Assemble committee members information kit. Mail committee members invitation letter for their meeting in week 14.		

transferred to the new, the new names received can be added, and the lists can be sorted to weed out the duplicates. The result will be two *uncorrupted*, usable databases.

CONCLUSION

This chapter provides tools that can be used for reverse networking. The end result is the recruitment of an event chair and co-chairs who would do the most good for the event and thus the nonprofit. These chairs then recruit the members of the event committee. As pointed out in Chapter 3 (Exhibit 3.3, Estimating Attendance), the more members on the event committee, the better chance the event will have to succeed in reaching its goals. This chapter links directly with Chapter 4, which details the structure that needs to be put in place to execute the networking and recruitment. In fact, Chapters 1, 2, 3, 4, 5, and 6 are codependent; when the steps outlined in these chapters are carried out, the seven goals can be accomplished. These core chapters also can assist nonprofits in their other fund-raising programs, all of which require organization of lay leadership.

CHAPTER SIX

Marketing

A DEFINITION AND INTRODUCTION TO SPECIAL EVENT MARKETING

For-profit marketers will define marketing as: The exchange of something of value for something you need, thus marketing is an exchange of goods and services for value.

Nonprofits define marketing as a process designed to bring about the voluntary exchange of values between a nonprofit organization and its target market, such as the transfer of a donation in exchange for addressing a social need, recognition, or a feeling of good will.[1]

A short, clear, and concise definition that applies to both profit and nonprofit organization is, find a need and fill it! For many years Kaiser Cement Corporation used a variation on its big mixer trucks: "Find a hole and fill it."

Applying either of the above definitions to nonprofit special event means, "that marketing the event can in turn apply to all programs of the nonprofit."

Nonprofit organizations view the marketing process from a different angle. Value is the key word, and "exchange" is used to describe fund raising and a fee for service, usually areas not available in the for-profit world. The "something" of value is the service the nonprofit is providing to the community. Many times the nonprofit organizations provide services to the recipients free of charge or for a fee so small it is only a fraction of the actual cost to the agency. Special events are one of many fund-raising programs agencies use to make up the difference in revenue. Marketing, as explained in this chapter, comprises the most creative thinking and work that can be accomplished by the professional staff and volunteers of a nonprofit agency. Both lay leaders and professional staff are involved in fund raising and achieving the entire seven goals; thus, by extension they are involved in the marketing process of a special event.

1. Raise Money
2. Update the Mission Statement to Educate Your Constituency
3. Motivate Board Members and Major Givers
4. Recruit Volunteers and Future Board Members
5. Expand the Organization's Network
6. Market the Organization
7. Solicit Endorsements

Phillip Kotler is a professor at Northwestern University's Kellog Graduate School of Management, and the author of the definitive work on nonprofit marketing, *Strategic Marketing for Non-Profit Institutions,* published in 1971. The following quotation is taken from an interview Kotler had with Peter Drucker (Drucker 1990, p. 84) summarizes the definition of nonprofit marketing: "Marketing is a way to harmonize the needs and wants of the outside world with the purposes and the resources and the objectives of the institution."[2] A special event is an excellent harmonizer as it is one of the few fund-raising programs that, if conducted intelligently, can bring together the outside world—the potential supporters—with the nonprofit's mission and the people, both volunteer lay leadership and professional staff.

IDENTIFYING THE MARKET

A definition of marketing usually continues with a list of tasks to be performed so that the organization—profit and nonprofit—can make intelligent decisions on the correct marketing strategy and vehicle. The vehicles are segmenting, targeting, and positioning; these vehicles are serviced by research and study of the market. In this case, the vehicle is a special event fund-raising program as applied to a specific nonprofit agency and its natural constituency.

Research and study of the nonprofit's market is an ongoing process for a heads-up agency. After defining its natural constituency—the supporters who originally funded and volunteered to start the agency—an organization must continue (on a daily basis) to prospect for the future lay leaders and donors. The fuel that keeps fund raising going and is essential for special events is building and adding to the mailing list. One reason why special events are popular with many agencies is because each provides them with new names of potential donors. How is this done? Every time a new event is produced, new event chairs, co-chairs, and committee members are recruited and they bring with them new names: the lifeblood of nonprofit agencies.

Segmenting, Targeting, and Positioning. For the special event, gathering the research means dividing the list into sublists that will be used to target specific constituencies. Even homogeneous lists—that is, names from a specific sector of potential supporters—can be segmented. For example, a list of law firms and their partners and associates should be filtered down into constituent parts: filtering out the partners, their specialties, and the associates. Such segmentation is easily accomplished with today's computers and sophisticated database programs.

Positioning primarily relates to the marketing of the nonprofit's programs or, more precisely, where the program(s) stand in relation to each other and, if applicable, to similar plans of other nonprofits. It specifically relates to special events in the sense that fund-raising events should be held on a date when there is the least competition from the fund-raising programs of other agencies. Nonprofits also have to avoid scheduling special events during the holiday season between Thanksgiving and Christmas, on long holiday weekends, and, in particular, when community members traditionally take vacations. For example, do not schedule a nationwide event for Alaska in the winter. Everyone who can afford to attend the event will choose a warm climate to vacation in. Even people who live in moderate climates travel during the winter, so agencies should check carefully with their lay leadership when setting dates or time periods to hold their special event.

A more traditional example of marketing positioning refers to the type of event the agency plans to produce. The Introduction describes a unique event, Dinner à la Heart. If an agency creates a distinct event— one like no other in the community—it can sew up the market for that special type of event. This is known as niche marketing. Smaller nonprofits that want to take advantage of the benefits of special events but are knocking heads with much larger organizations that produce three or four special events each year tend to focus on unique events. Smaller agencies can produce a boutique-type event and even draw supporters from other agencies' events.

KEY MARKETING WORDS AND ACTIONS

How can a nonprofit special event be marketed? The following key concepts should be kept in mind as a marketing plan is created:

- Identification
- Values
- Programs
- Communication
- Training
- Public Relations
- Implementation

Identification

The agency's and the special event's name must be placed in the forefront of all activities associated with this particular project; include the agency's address, identifying logo, telephone and fax number, e-mail address, and Web site name.

Values

The mission statement explains what the organization does and how it does it. The statement explains the effect these actions and programs have on the agency's natural constituency and community. Use it!

Programs

The agency's programs and the services it provides to the community must be identified with the agency's name and logo. An agency with more than two or three programs should use a graphic illustration so the targeted constituency can associate the organization concretely.

Communication

Advertising and public relations communicate purpose to the constituency. Nonprofits generally use print media (with radio and the Internet a close second, and television somewhat down on the list due to its cost). Agencies commonly use the following types of communication: the special event's save-the-date mailing, formal invitations, business cards with all the pertinent information about the event printed on them, newspaper press releases (public press and in-house publications), radio, television, posters, billboards (only for high-end special events), and e-mail and the World Wide Web.

Training

Training a volunteer is training a marketer! Volunteers come from various segments of the community. Even when they are not actually working in the agency's office or program site, they continue spreading information about the nonprofit by telling its story to their friends and wherever they interact with people. (Make sure the volunteers have an ample supply of business cards detailing important special events.)

Public Relations

Special event committee members, chairperson(s), and the nonprofit's executive director are the agency's most knowledgeable people. They know the agency and the particulars of the event. When possible, schedule them at press conferences, service club meetings, and any venue where there are potential supporters and event attendees.

Every special event generates its own public relations materials. These include:

- The save-the-date card
- The letter to join the event committee
- The personal letter from the committee member to potential guests
- The special event's formal invitation

The above marketing materials apply to all of the constituencies where public relations will help the nonprofit: the general community, specialized professions, and the agency's natural constituency.

Implementation

Marketing is a verb! Verbs denote action. Action is a strategic marketing plan put into play by tactics. (Remember, for nonprofits, "tactics" means people.)

A SPECIAL EVENT'S MARKETING PLAN

Exhibit 4.1 in Chapter 4 outlines the people required to activate the marketing strategy; the integration of people with the marketing plan just described will result in the implementation of the philosophy of the seven goals; and finally, marketing tasks are listed as to-do items in the METT. Graphically, it looks like the following:

PHILOSOPHY   *STRATEGY*   *TACTICS*   *TIME LINE*

Seven Goals → Marketing Plan → Implementers → METT

The special event succeeds because the tactics succeed. Remember, in nonprofit fund raising, "tactics" means "people." In Exhibit 6.1, almost all of the people listed under "Who is responsible" are the leaders: agency executive board members, event chair and co-chairs, and lay leadership. Successful leaders work in the trenches! They solicit support from their peers, corporations, and public and private foundations. By working this way, they motivate the event committee members, the agency's board members, large supporters of the nonprofit, and everyone they can talk to. Planning strategy is needed, but tactics make the wheels turn. This is a variant on Al Ries and Jack Trout's theory of bottom-up marketing,[3] which is the opposite of traditional fundraising practice that preaches the "tip-of-iceberg," top-down solicitation theory. Top-down solicitation is correct for one-on-one, major gift, and capital gift strategies; but, as outlined in Chapter 4, a solid base must be constructed for special events. Once the tactical troops are recruited, then the upward push to the rewards of underwriters, sponsors, table purchases, and journal advertisements can be achieved.

Developing and executing a general marketing program for the nonprofit is not an overnight task. It requires patience, goals, research, strategy, and tactics that usually take years, not months. A marketing plan for a special event must be executed in a much shorter time. Using the METT as a guide, start planning the event marketing strategy no later than the fourth week in the 27-week cycle. A first priority of the event chair should be the recruitment of a professional marketing and public relations and/or advertising executive for the marketing co-chair position. Use Exhibit 4.7, the Special Event Case Statement (Chapter 4), to help recruit this co-chair. One of the documents in that case statement is the marketing plan; either use the generic shown in Exhibit 6.1 or begin to formulate a basic strategy based on this model that can be shown to prospective co-chairs. Candidates usually are impressed by the fact that an agency has devoted time and energy to this plan; recruitment becomes that much easier.

A SPECIAL EVENT MARKETING PLAN—EXAMPLE

This example will be based on a testimonial award dinner. This type of event is the most difficult to market because it is put on so frequently by so many organizations that it is frequently referred to as the "rubber chicken" dinner. Testimonial award dinners also lack the appeal and energy of an auction or athletic tournament; the pizzazz of a symphony, ballet, theater, or opera opening night; or the glamour of a fancy dress ball, complete with celebrities. If your nonprofit can market a testimonial event and gain the community awareness necessary for success (a sell out crowd), then it is ready to tackle the more complex and sophisticated special events. However, an organization will suffer no loss of pride or purpose to being the nonprofit organization in the community that produces the most successful yearly testimonial dinner, and by doing so, achieves the pot of gold at the end of the Seven Goals, which are the bedrock philosophy of this book (see the Introduction). To accomplish and implement the marketing plan outlined in this chapter, the following items must be accomplished by the nonprofit:

Exhibit 6.1   Executing the Marketing Plan for a Special Event

Marketing Plan Objective	Strategy	Who Is Responsible	Outcome(s)
Recruit Volunteers	Establish objectives from Exhibits 4.2 to 4.4	Agency's board and development committee	Organize event committee
Raise Money	Establish gross and net $ to be raised and attendance	Event chair and agency professional	Determine amount of funds to be raised
Mission Statement	Educate and motivate guests	Event committee members and agency staff	Guests become aware of the work of the nonprofit; defines non-monetary objectives
Implementation	Put into action seven goals philosophy	Board members, event chair, and co-chairs (with assistance from honorary chairs)	New supporters are introduced to the nonprofit's leadership; they are candidates for stewardship
Constituency	Execute networking plan (Chapter 5)	Agency leadership and event chairs and co-chairs event committee members	Expanded invitation list; clean up existing list(s)
Identification	Research all potential sources that can reach the targeted constituency (see communications objective)	Co-chair in charge of public relations, event chair, and staff professional	Secure media exposure for the event, (who, what, why, when, where)
Values	Communicate nonprofit's Mission Statement to constituency & community. Define nonprofit's niche and value to community	Honorary chairs with the help of lay leadership and professional staff	Nonprofit is recognized as the primary provider of their special services and programs to community
Funds and Friends	Plan the strategy to identify sources of financial support; make it easy for everyone to support the agency	Event chairs in conjunction with event committee members and agency lay leadership	Meet special event fund-raising goals; realistic ratio of revenue versus expenses (See Chapter 3)

Exhibit 6.1 *(continued)*

Marketing Plan Objective	Strategy	Who Is Responsible	Outcome(s)
Communication	Use all avenues to obtain mention of the special event in in-house and external publications, radio, T.V., posters and handouts, etc.	P.R. chair in conjunction with event chair, lay leadership, and professional staff.	Agency's special event becomes the "event" to attend through mention in all types of media and word-of-mouth networking

Define Goal: The theoretical organization's budget in Chapter 3 indicates its goal is to raise $100,500 in gross revenue from its event and to attract 670 people to the testimonial dinner. Based on its results from completing Exhibit 2.1, it needs to complete the following tasks to achieve its goals: motivate at least 20 of 25 board members to get them active with the special event; recruit at least 60 active volunteers to work on the event and other agency programs; expand the agency's network of names to at least 2,500; increase the active contributor list to 1,250; develop marketing plan to highlight the agency throughout the county; update the mission statement to address agency's new county-wide programming; and solicit endorsements by corporate and local governments VIP's. The people will arrive as guests, but leave as friends and future supporters of the agency.

Identify: The organization needs to define its constituency and invite them. Whoever is in charge of marketing must make it his or her business to investigate every path presented to them by their current supporters. An educational institution invites its alumni. A religious institution invites its members and asks them to invite friends who are also members of the same denomination. A hospital invites physicians and the supporting medical technologists. In many situations, the entire community benefits from the nonprofit's work, so members of the community at large are invited. In addition, there is often a constituency within a constituency. For example, a congregation that has a large membership from one profession has those members network with other professionals from that area who do not belong to the congregation, but who would support one of the church's programs, for example, helping the hungry. The motto is: Leave no stone unturned—there is gold in them thar hills!

Communication: The organization must prepare a press release (see Special Resources, p. 202) when the event is first announced, highlighting all of the goals that the special event was designed to achieve—the first salvo in the bombardment of communications prepared to inform the community of the agency's plans. Use the following publications to promote the event:

- The organization's monthly newsletter
- A newspaper editorial or letter to the editor of the local newspaper—daily, weekly, and professional publications
- Save-the-date announcement
- Letters to prominent community citizens (See Chapter 4)
- Formal invitations (See Chapter 1)
- Special business cards to be handed out by members (See Exhibit 6.2)
- A special fact sheet for electronic transmissions:
  1. E-mail
  2. Facsimile

Implementation: The event committee members must implement the special event plan. Their job as committee members is twofold: First, to sell tables, seats, and advertisements for the program journal; second, to market the nonprofit agency. In order to sell anything, a marketing person must know the "product," and the nonprofit's product is detailed in their Mission Statement.

The committee should develop detailed plans (see communications paragraph) to identify its organization and the event. For example, "Alpha Philanthropic presents a testimonial dinner honoring The Phil-

Exhibit 6.2   Special Event Business Card

1st ANNUAL ADL CIVIL RIGHTS LUNCHEON
Monday, June 30, 1997
11:30-1:30
Fairmont Hotel
Couvert: $50.00

Keynote Speaker:
Abraham Foxman
National Director of the Anti-Defamation League
For reservations call (415) 981-3500

anthropist of the Year at the Posh Hotel on the hill. It will be held on Sunday evening, May 31, 1998, from 6:30 P.M. to 9:30 P.M." This must be repeated as frequently as possible in as many mediums as possible; one of the ways to do this is with the use of the business card, Exhibit 6.2. The business card is easy for everyone involved with the event to use: easy to carry and fun to hand out to the committee member's friends and associates.

To further implement the special event and, by doing so, motivate its lay leaders and volunteers, the agency will outline its values which is its niche in the community. For example, the organization provides a clean bed and dinner for more homeless people in the community than any other nonprofit agency. This is a value all volunteers and current supporters (and potential supporters) involved with the agency can be proud of, and which the organization can ethically highlight to raise funds to continue these projects. The agency should answer the questions most present or future supporters may have: Who or what will be effected by the mission of the nonprofit? Where do the effected people or groups live in the community?

When preparing the press releases and fact sheets suggested above, describing the agency's mission in the community and how this event will further that mission, the board of director's names as well as those supporting the major foundation and public agencies are mentioned or attached as an addendum to the press release and fact sheet.

Also part of the implementation process is what is termed: "Funds and Friends." This information that can be outlined in the fact sheet describes the facts about how much the agency wishes to raise and techniques to interest the new people who support the event so that they become regular supporters and contributors. Use information from Chapter 3, the Event Budget, Exhibit 3.1, which describes how much the event will raise in gross revenue, how much the expenses will cost, and how people and outside organizations can participate. Will there be a program journal with paid advertisements? Will there be an opportunity to purchase advertisements and tables for a reduced package price? Remember, there are no secrets in a well run nonprofit, all information must be accurate and available to the public.

RIDING THE INTERNET WAVE

For the past few years no self-respecting organization, nonprofit, or for-profit would consider itself a "with-it" marketer if it did not have a Web site. Web sites (www.organization's name or abbreviation.web extension) are a legitimate and easy way to get a message across to thousands of people, if they know where to look. The agency's Web address and the key words to describe it only go so far and can place it among hundreds of other organizations when they are input into a search engine. One way to overcome this is to advertise a Web address on letterhead, business cards, and every piece of printed material that is meant for the public. A small ad in the local newspaper or the nonprofit's professional periodical also will lead viewers to the nonprofit's web site.

While Web sites can be used for many purposes, our focus is special events. Web sites can promote events and can provide a direct link via e-mail for the browser to make a reservation, donation, or purchase an advertisement in the program journal. As an added incentive, the agency can hold a preevent auction on the site. For example, say a cruise ship line has donated a trip for two on one of its popular ships or to promote a new ship. The agency establishes a minimum bid price, outlines all of the terms of the auction, and sets a final date for bids to be entered. The auction can be promoted in all of the event documents: save-the-date, press releases, on the letterhead, and on formal invitations. The winner could be announced at the event. All types of items can be auctioned on the Web. But, like all successful fund-raising programs, these auctions need to be planned!

GETTING YOUR MESSAGE TO THE MEDIA

Public relations (PR) can be a subtle form of promotion one minute, and brash the next. A one-dimensional definition of the term means that the agency tries to get a media source to mention their new program (saying good things about it) on a television news segment, on the radio, or an article in the news media. A more comprehensive definition is the activity of developing public awareness among opinion leaders and the general public and in return the attitude of the public toward an organization.[3]

Planting these news gems is the work of professionals who use their personal contacts to gain access with the media. Personal contacts are only one-half of the equation; the other half is the press release. Press releases are written in many forms: Low key, low key and subtle, matter of fact, and the headline, bold announcement type. Nonprofits are usually at or near the bottom of the food chain in getting space or a good word mentioned in the media, so the bold announcement type of press release is the only way most agencies can hope to receive any recognition from a media editor. But, even if the editor notices the nonprofit's press release, it has to be well written, and in the five "Ws" format: Who, what, why, when, and where! The resource section includes an example of a bold, five "Ws" press release (see p. 202).

If the organization does not have an in-house PR professional, try to recruit one through networking as explained in Chapter 4, and make the person a co-chair; the next best situation is to arrange with one of the event chair(s) who is associated with a large corporation to lend the agency some time from their PR department; the third suggestion is to have the event chair (or other chair(s) or co-chair(s)) to solicit a special contribution to cover the cost of hiring a PR firm. A creative PR professional can do wonders for the event in obtaining recognition for the event by using the agency's mission statement and further, by clearly explaining the agency's various programs to the public.

If the nonprofit is located in a metropolitan area where the community is spread out, but does most of its business in a hub city—Chicago, Denver, New York, Miami, San Francisco, Los Angeles—the event message needs to be "seeded" in all of the areas. Contact one of the news distribution services, e.g., *Business Wire*. A 400 word text-only article can be distributed at a nonprofit rate of under $100. A few minutes of investigation in your area will provide all the details.

METT Checklist for Chapter 6

Week	·	To Do This Week	Book Ref.	☑
4		Prepare preliminary marketing plan		
5 through 25		Execute marketing and public relations plan Coordinate all mailings and public documents: Save the date card, committee recruitment letters, formal invitations, press releases, media information kit, and committee members personal invitation letters.		

CONCLUSION

Using proven marketing strategies and adopting them to the special event is at the core of this chapter. Definitions, key marketing tasks, and key words and actions lead to a comprehensive marketing plan and the execution of that plan. Marketing is one of the seven goals for a special event and is a crucial strategy in explaining the nonprofit's values to the community. Using the special event as one of the vehicles to get that message across is at the core of an excellent fund-raising plan.

NOTES

[1]Peter F. Drucker, *Managing the Nonprofit Organization: Principal and Practices.* (New York: HarperCollins, 1990), p. 84.
[2]Ibid.
[3]Al Ries and Jack Trout, *Bottom-up Marketing.* (New York: McGraw-Hill, 1989.)
[4]Barbara R. Levy and R. L. Cherry, (eds.), *The NSFRE Fund-Raising Dictionary.* (New York: John Wiley & Sons, 1996.)

CHAPTER SEVEN

Special Event Administration

INTRODUCTION

Goals, planning, and organizing are three of the four pillars required to produce a successful special event. Administration is the 4th pillar. Attention to details, which is why there is that tiresome animal, the checklist, and its siblings the agenda, time line, and worksheet, enables event administrators and managers to achieve success. Allowing an agency to produce a gala celebration, a fun testimonial, or a sports tournament without a detailed plan squanders the funds the nonprofit is endeavoring to raise.

The old adage is true: Success is in the details!

THE FIRST CONCERNS: LOCATION, FOOD, AND SERVICE

Location is a prime consideration in putting on a special event. Many times, the location chooses itself because of factors that are beyond the organization's control. Even in large metropolitan locations, where there are many locations to select from, the agency is sometimes directed to one hotel over another. This can happen for a variety of reasons, including: The hotel's senior management is active with the nonprofit and sits on the board of directors and will make the production of the event much easier to put on, both in price and staff consideration; the hotel's staff is unionized, and your agency is located in a predominantly union community (and many of your supporters are union members); or the hotel or club is set-up to provide special features, such as a kosher kitchen or a large dining area combined with a golf or tennis facility.

Decoration of the event site can also be a consideration in choosing one venue over another, e.g., if your event features a circus theme and the agency wants to "redecorate" the main ballroom and even bring in animals, the availability of sites can become restricted. There may be only one or two to choose from in your community.

Special entertainment beyond the usual dance band or string trio brought in to provide background music, can also be a factor in the selection of a site. If your plan calls for a rock concert, you are probably going to have to select the largest auditorium in the community, or even arrange to hold it outdoors, which requires permits from the city or county and the governing police force. This brings up the subject of security, which some agencies must arrange for because of their special mission in the community, which brings out local pickets and/or unknown potential problems. If your guest keynote speaker is a prominent national or international personality or celebrity, then the agency has to provide security. Security can be arranged through the hiring of off-duty local police or sheriff deputies, or from private security agencies that provide trained licensed personnel.

If you are hiring extra people or have an extraordinary number of volunteers, plan to feed them. This can be accomplished in one of two ways: either have them fill-in at tables that have empty seats because of no shows (after all the agency has guaranteed a certain number of dinners, and it is a shame to pay for food that is not consumed) or, in your planning with the catering manager, have a separate section set-up for the support staff, security people, and others that will be assisting at the event, but will not be taking part in it.

The Master Event Timetable (METT) starts off week 6 with, "negotiations with site and catering managers are begun." Hotels usually have only one person who must be negotiated with; however, if your event is to be catered at a site where everything must be brought in, then there can be two individuals to negotiate with: The site manager and the catering manager. This is the most important contract. It obligates the agency and the vendor organization, e.g., hotel, caterer, country club, or any other entity that promises to provide a service. Exhibits 7.1 (CH0701.DOC) and 7.2 are designed for an off-site catering event, but they can be easily modified for use with an event that is held in a hotel or restaurant that has adequate seating.

When meeting the catering manager for the first time, make sure he or she knows the organization's status as a nonprofit agency. Give the manager all the particulars regarding the event: Date, time, estimated number of guests that will attend, whether a pre-luncheon or dinner reception will be held for different categories of supporters, security required for special guests, and any other pertinent items. Special requests should be brought up at the initial meeting, not later as a surprise second thought. Negotiating the lowest price means that both sides have to start out on a level playing field. After the catering manager has looked at the whole picture, he or she can make a realistic quotation—then the negotiations can begin. If more than one possible site is being considered, someone from the agency should telephone those sites and obtain nonbinding pricing information that can be used for comparison purposes. Most venues go out of their way to book events from nonprofit agencies; however, some sites are indifferent or just want to do business with for-profit organizations. The initial reception by the catering manager will set the tone of the conversation—it will be evident whether the business is wanted. Remember, if the event is marketed correctly, the venue, the hotel, or the catering facility can receive good public relations, which it can use in their marketing efforts. Negotiations should be conducted in the spirit of "getting to yes." The site was chosen because of some characteristics that the committee thought were advantageous to the event, so do not let negotiations deteriorate into a shouting match. Tell the catering manager who is involved with the event. If by chance these people are prominent in the community, then a "hook" has been established that can be used throughout the negotiation process. The manager can justify a no-charge here and a reduction there, and in the end both parties are winners. If the catering manager is excited about the agency and the event, that enthusiasm will be transferred to the rest of the team and that can only mean a better and more successful event.

There are a lot of blank lines that must be filled in so that the agency can receive all of the special items it needs to create a unique event. The following Exhibit 7.1, although not inclusive, itemizes the generic requirements most agencies need and should consider for their events.

Exhibit 7.1   Catering Specifications: List

Food and Ambiance	*Logistics*
Menu Choices • Hors d'oeuvres, salads, entrée, dessert, and beverage(s) • Notations on what not to serve if there are any dietary restrictions, e.g., if your agency is devoted to vegetarianism, it would not be a good idea to serve miniature hot dogs hors d'oeuvres. • Silverware and china • Crystal or plastic glasses • Color of linen and table coverings • Table centerpiece (what is included: candles, flowers, ice carving, or miniature flags, etc.) and what the agency and the site (caterer/ restaurant/hotel) provides • Corkage fee (if applicable)	• Price per guest meal based on agency's minimum guarantee; advance time for final guarantee (usually 72 hours prior to event) • Percentage increase fluctuation from base guaranteed attendance. For example, most hotels prepare enough food for a 5 percent increase in attendance. • Size of round tables: 60 inches or 72 inches • Specification of which space facility the agency is reserving. Detail the conditions under which the facility can be switched (only with prior approval) • Graphic drawing of room showing the position of each table, the stage and podiums, check-in tables, and coat racks if there is no separate coat room • Cancellation policy: Number of days prior to the event that the organization can cancel without incurring a fee based on the original number of guests and the per-person charge • Audiovisual setup: Who is responsible? Is this billed separately?

Exhibit 7.2 is a bid prepared with the above list in mind.

Exhibit 7.2   Catering Specifications

Catering Specifications
for
125th Anniversary Celebration Reception
Thursday, November 6, 1998
5:30 p.m. to 7:30 p.m.
Prepare a bid for a minimum of 750 guests
and a maximum of 1,000 guests

Site: Merchants Exchange Building Ballroom—15th Floor
465 California Street, San Francisco
See attached floor plan for Ballroom, Bar and Reception area
Sq. Ft. = 5,735

Small station buffets (preferred):
- Indicate number of stations
- Items to be served: (cold and hot)
- Seafood, chicken, turkey, meat (describe menu at each station):
  1. Salad(s)—describe menu
  2. Accompanying food for above—breads, sauces, pate, cheeses, etc.

Passed hors d'oeuvres (number of servers assigned)
- Indicate number and description of hors d'oeuvres, i.e., fish, poultry, vegetarian, meat, and cheese

Provide and serve soft drinks and mineral water by station; indicate number of stations.

Caterer to provide coffee and light desserts at indicated stations.

Client to provide own wine, caterer to serve. There will be no hard liquor. (Explain your corkage policy and indicate a price inclusive of service charge and tax.)

Floral decoration needed for buffet and cocktail tables.

Outline equipment provided (glassware, utensils, and linen, etc.).

Indicate number and description of service personnel—break down by station and butler-style service.

Break down catering costs by category and be inclusive; please show service charge, sales tax and total:

Show separately—floral, lighting, coat check, valet parking, and restroom attendants expense.

Caterers: Provide a taste sampling of selected items at client's office.

Mail quotation to: Staff executive in charge of event. Indicate agency address, telephone, fax, and e-mail address.

IMPORTANT PEOPLE

Whether holding an event at a hotel, conference center facility, or a restaurant, the people listed in Exhibit 7.3, an organization chart for a typical food and beverage department, are the ones who can make or break the event.

Although the closest association will be with the catering manager, the No. 1 person in the hotel's food and beverage department is the director; in fact, the planner should make a point of meeting this person. A personal call to the director often can smooth out a lot of ruffles; catering managers change jobs frequently. If this happens in the middle of the event timetable, knowing the director on a first-name basis would be advantageous.

NEGOTIATING POINTS IN CONTRACTS

The most important contract is the one that obligates the agency and the venue organization, e.g., hotel, caterer, country club, and any entity that promises to provide a service for the nonprofit. Hotel and catering contracts are standard documents, varying usually with the difference in state and local laws where they are written.

During the first week, the METT instructs the planner to choose the site and set the date for the event. The planner has confirmed this in writing; now it is time to start plans with the people concerned.

If the event is going to be held annually rather than just once every three to five years, then the venue site will have an interest in working more closely with an organization. Top hotels, for example, are very interested in showing off catering expertise, so that they can market their facilities to the guests for their life-cycle events—weddings, confir-

Exhibit 7.3   A Typical Food and Beverage Department

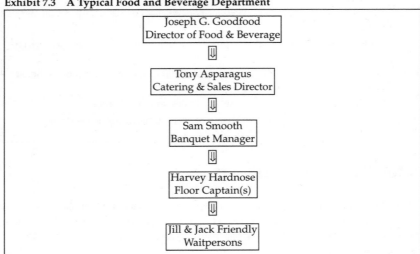

mations, anniversaries, and the like. In addition, the nonprofit organization may want to negotiate based on the following points:

- The number of guests can be a factor since the chef can purchase items in quantity for a better price and pass along the savings to the nonprofit.
- If the wine is donated, corkage is an excellent item for a negotiated lower price.
- Locally obtainable items are less expensive than imported or exotic foods grown or caught in faraway places like halfway around the world.
- Unless your community has a water quality problem, use tap water instead of the bottled variety.
- Try to offer only one main entrée, either fish or beef, with a vegetarian option for non–meat eaters.
- Suggest that the hotel or caterer sponsor dessert in return for acknowledgment in the event program and/or tent cards on each table.

Exhibit 7.4 is an example of a completed contract for an event.

EVENT STAFFING REQUIREMENTS

For special events that include a sit-down meal or buffet, the one thing that should not be skimped on is the number of service staff. Professional staff required to administer an event can range from three to twelve people for a testimonial dinner/dance with an auction. If the agency is small, with only a few staff members, then the professional staff will have to recruit volunteers from the board of directors to help at the event. If there are going to be 250 guests at dinner, the facility will usually suggest one banquet captain who will supervise two waitpersons for every four tables of ten. The facility probably will not agree to anything less than this minimum figure; it does not want to get a reputation for slow service. Besides, union rules may dictate the ratio that is allowed. If a lengthy program is scheduled for after the meal, it is sometimes advisable to pay extra and lower the ratio to two waitpersons for every three tables of ten.

Receptions are different. Many have buffet tables and passed hors d'oeuvres. The suggested ratios for these events are: 1 hors d'oeuvres passer for every 40 guests; 3 service people per buffet station: 2 servers and 1 runner assigned per station for every 100 guests. Busers for receptions gather the used glasses and plates at a ratio of 1 per 200 guests for

Exhibit 7.4   Sample Catering Contract

October 30, 1997

<u>CONTRACT #4493—Revised 1</u>
<u>(Page One of Two)</u>

ALPHA

Fine Catering   RE: Fundraising Event

Event Production   Event Data: Thursday, November 6, 1997
                       5:30–7:30 PM
                       Full Service Catering, 1,100 guests
                       Event Site: Merchants Exchange Building, San Francisco

Consulting   *FOOD SERVICE:*
                       —Beautifully presented Passed Hors d'oeuvres and Buffet
                         Stations
                       —Dark Roast Coffee Service
                       —Complete event set-up, maintenance and breakdown

                       SERVICE STAFF (based on a Two Hour Event)*:
                       —(1) Chef
                       —(11) Kitchen Staff
                       —(1) Scullery
                       —(1) Event Manager
                       —(21) Buffet/Floor Attendants
                       —(2) Bussers

                       *Service staff fees included are based on an 5.5 hour shift,
                       including set-up and clean-up from staff arrival (2.5 hours
                       prior to event) to staff departure (1 hour after event). Should
                       the client request an extension of these hours, additional
                       charges will incur: $30 per Chef and Event Manager; $22 per
                       hour for Kitchen Staff, Buffet Attendants and Bar Staff (listed
                       under "Beverage Service"): $15 per Busser and Scullery.

                       EQUIPMENT:
                       —Buffet tables with linens
                       —Small china plates, small forks, glass coffee mugs, paper
                         cocktail napkins
                       —All necessary catering/kitchen equipment
                       —*Seating tables and chairs to be determined*

                       BUFFET TABLE-TOP DECOR AND STYLING:
                       —Thematic buffet table design/decor, installation and
                         styling labor, as well as Now We're Cooking! platters,
                         bowls, baskets, utensils, fabrics, props, etc.

Exhibit 7.4 *(continued)*

Fine Catering	*BEVERAGE SERVICE (based on a Two Hour Event):* —(11) Bar Staff —Assorted Soft Drinks, Sparkling Water —All necessary bar equipment, glassware, ice, condiments —Complete bar set-up, maintenance and breakdown —*All wine provided by client*
Event Production	—*Advance site inspection, consultations, layout, logistics and planning meetings all included in total cost*
Consulting	*GRAND TOTAL* $33,517.00 Add: (10) kiosk/linens (@ $26 ea.) $260.00 8.50% Sales Tax $22.10 Deposit Received (11,425.00) *FINAL BALANCE DUE 11/6/97* $22,374.10 *—All Inclusive Package Price—* NOTE: GRAND TOTAL INCLUDES SALES TAX. *NOTE: THIS PRICE IS BASED ON VOLUME; SHOULD THE GUARANTEED GUEST COUNT BE REDUCED TO LESS THAN 1,100 GUESTS, APPROPRIATE PER PERSON COST ADJUSTMENTS MAY BE MADE.* *FINAL BALANCE DUE DAY OF EVENT—Thank You!*

Used with permission from now we're cooking! Caterers, San Francisco.

paper and plastic items and 1 per 100 guests for china and glass. A clean and neat reception area is vital.

Golf tournaments and other sports events require the nonprofit to provide at least 12 support staff, plus three senior staff members.

Don't Be Stingy with Waitpersons

At one of this writer's first events, given at a well-known hotel in the community (part of a national chain), waitpersons ignored the front-row corner table. I did not notice this happening, but fortunately a friend alerted me to the situation, although too late to do anything about it. (I had been occupied with some other arrangements on the opposite end of the ballroom; the lesson taught me that an event also can have too few staff people.) While I was rounding up the banquet captain, eight of the ten guests seated at the table got up and left en masse. (My two friends remained, as a courtesy to me.) At this point, my only recourse was to talk to the catering director, who had gone home for the evening. After scorching him over the telephone and making an appointment for the next morning, my parting words were "Bring your checkbook." For the remainder of the evening, I personally directed the wait staff and the banquet captain and made sure that everything was served on time to all of the guests at each table. The next morning I met with the catering manager and came away with a substantial discount, over half of the entire invoice. My next telephone calls were to the eight guests who had left to offer them an apology and a refund. (They were gracious enough to understand the situation and declined the refund offer.) The point: Always make sure there is ample staff for an event; do this by making sure that the catering manager, banquet manager, and floor captain and professional staff agree on the ratio of servers to guest tables. And, as mentioned, have adequate staff and/or volunteers from the agency assisting the event planner in monitoring the site. In today's world of high-tech electronics, almost everyone has a cellular telephone for large outside events. For indoor, ballroom events an agency can rent at reasonable prices two or three walkie-talkies. Like marketing, there is nothing like good floor communications.

DESIGNING THE SITE: WHERE TO PLACE THE TABLES AND PODIUMS

Chapter 8 describes how to seat guests in detail. Before seating guests, however, the site must be designed. Many readers have attended large events where over 250 guests have been seated or 500 to 1,000 guests have been fed and served cocktails at a reception. It looks so simple from the guests' perspective; however, forethought and planning are needed to reach this level of simplicity. The two basic types of special events that need this planning are testimonials and receptions—that is, sit-down or stand-up events. Since most special events feed or serve food of some type, the agency's event planner should be greatly interested in how to set the site up for maximum efficiency, if for no other reason than because preplanning will make the event seem effortless, which in turn will make the guests go home and tell their friends what a great event they attended.

What not to do when setting up a ballroom for a sit-down dinner is design the room (design = table placement), in a rectangular or square configuration, with a group of tables and a raised head table on one of the room's sides. All of the VIPs are seated at the head table looking down at the guests who soon feel like victims in the Coliseum, especially when the speeches begin and the lions start to roar. In fact such a design reverses the true order of the event: It assumes that the VIPs are the important people at the event, whereas only the honoree(s) at the head table and the guests sitting at the tables are truly important. In this type of room design, there is very little interaction between guests and honoree(s); think about the situation where the honoree is sitting at the raised head table and can only be approached by the guests who want to wish them well, from below. Guests are straining their necks looking up, and the honoree(s) is in the awkward position of standing up and bending over the table (covered with food) and reaching down to shake hands. At best, this room design is uncomfortable.

There is a better method: the table-of-honor design seen in Exhibit 7.5.

The table of honor transfers the flow of the event from craning necks to the eye-to-eye meeting where everyone is comfortable. Instead of rectangles and squares, the room is designed in the round or oval. The table of honor is placed in the center of the dining area; depending on how many people are sitting there, the layout is either round or a large oval. The guests sit at tables in concentric rings placed around the table of honor (who sits where and closest is discussed in Chapter 8), and even those sitting in the outer ring have access and feel near the center of things. This room design gives everyone a feeling of inclusion where the guests can mingle with the honoree(s) and VIPs on a level playing field. This exhibit was printed from the Event Planner Plus™ program; more information on this program is in the resource section.

Exhibit 7.5   Table-of-Honor Ballroom Floor Plan

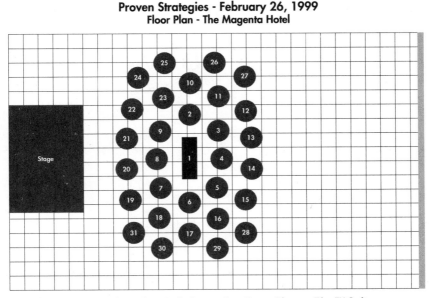

Used with permission from Certain Software, Inc. Event Planner Plus™ Software.

A stand-up reception (compared to a reception where there are adequate cocktail tables provided) presents different problems centered around feeding and serving guests who are more mobile than stationary. The placement of serving tables, small cocktail tables for guests, and tall platforms where guests can place a glass of wine and lean against is crucial.

Exhibit 7.6 is a graphic drawing/representation of a reception that includes music and dancing. The exhibit shows where each segment is placed in relationship to the dance floor and kitchen. It indicates where every table is located and defines a flow for the guests, e.g., there are

Exhibit 7.6   Small Dance Reception

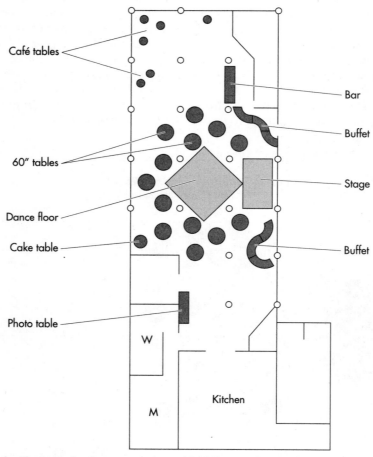

Used with permission from now we're cooking! Caterers, San Francisco.

two buffets, one on either side of the stage, and is designed for guests to sit at larger tables. At this reception, more than finger food is being served.

The buffet layout seen in Exhibit 7.7 is designed for finger food and for many guests who probably will eat and drink standing. The curved design serves two purposes: It shows the path around a large permanent pillar, which could be an obstruction, and it provides a flow scheme showing where guests can obtain food and beverages from either side of the buffet tables.

Exhibit 7.7   Individual Buffet Table Layouts

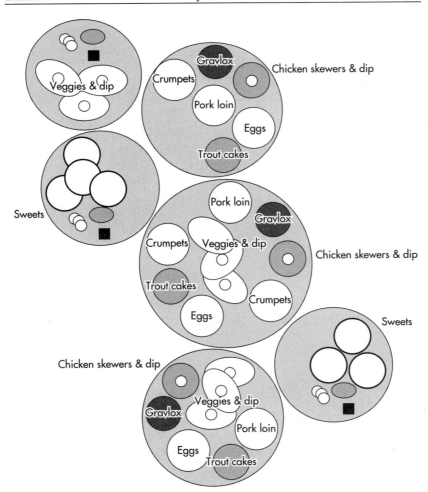

Used with permission from now we're cooking! Caterers, San Francisco.

Exhibit 7.8 shows the details of one of the buffet sections that could be used with Exhibit 7.4. Most guests will obtain food from one side of the carving buffet, although some may "attack" the other side.

Exhibit 7.9 is another example of the detailed layout of three different types of buffets and shows how to drape the tables for best advantage and ambience. Professional caterers will provide this detail; in effect, they plan every step guests take so that the flow of the reception proceeds as smoothly as possible. Even though a professional caterer will provide designs like these, the agency should prepare preliminary designs so that the caterer can visually understand what the agency desires for its event or reception.

Unless the organization or a member of the professional staff or a lay leader has worked with a particular caterer before and knows his or her reputation from a personal experience, check all the references the caterer provides. Assume that the references are from satisfied customers, but ask them a few judicious questions, such as:

1. Was the food and drink the same quality and freshness contracted for?
2. Was an ample quanty of all items available?
3. Was the hot food hot and the cold food cold?
4. Did the caterer arrive at the site on time and was the setup completed in time for a walk-through before the first guests arrived?
5. Were the waitpersons friendly and knowledgeable?
6. Was an event captain on duty throughout the event?

If earlier customers answer these questions positively, then the caterer is the real thing. Try to talk to at least two references. As mentioned previously, an event presents the agency to the public. When people go home or back to their offices and talk to friends and colleagues, what they say about the event will reflect on the agency. Of course, the agency wants all the statements to be positive.

POSTAL MATTERS

Before mailing any information about the event, consult the U.S. postal regulations to determine the most economical way to do so. Here are some of the various details that must be considered:

-   A nonprofit, bulk-mail indicia may save you money. "Indicia" is the post office term for the distinctive mark located in the

Exhibit 7.8   Twenty-Foot Carving Buffet

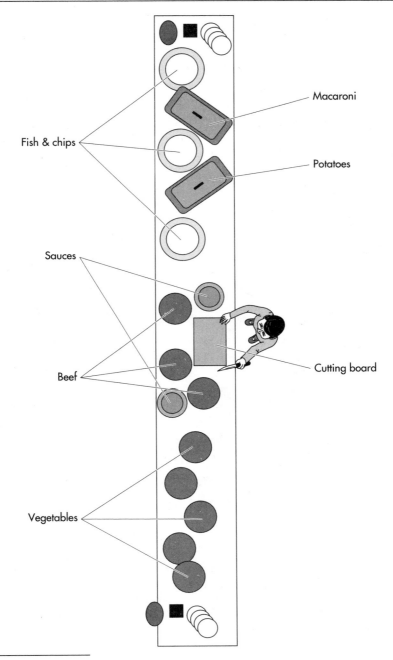

Macaroni

Fish & chips

Potatoes

Sauces

Cutting board

Beef

Vegetables

Used with permission from now we're cooking! Caterers, San Francisco.

Exhibit 7.9   Three Buffet Table Design

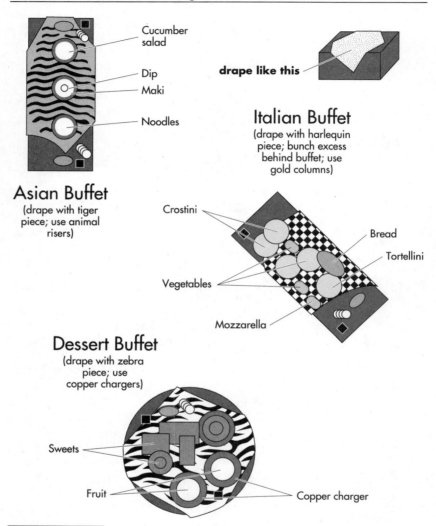

drape like this

Italian Buffet
(drape with harlequin
piece; bunch excess
behind buffet; use
gold columns)

Cucumber
salad

Dip

Maki

Noodles

Asian Buffet
(drape with tiger
piece; use animal
risers)

Crostini

Bread

Tortellini

Vegetables

Mozzarella

Dessert Buffet
(drape with zebra
piece; use
copper chargers)

Sweets

Fruit

Copper charger

Used with permission from now we're cooking! Caterers, San Francisco.

upper right-hand corner of the envelope, where the stamp
would be placed. The U.S. Postal Service (or USPS, as it now
likes to be known) sells permits to qualified nonprofits; see
postal publication #417 for details. The indicia is placed in a box
and reads: *Non Profit Organization/PAID/Name of your City,
State/Permit No. XXX.* A special nonprofit stamp can be used
instead of the indicia.

- The size of envelope determines the cost of postage. The post office has specific requirements that will affect the design of your mailing piece.
- Bulk mailings have specific timing parameters. The post office will provide this information, which must be followed exactly when using this economical mailing method.

For specifics, the USPS has an 800 number: 800-275-8777. It is also on the World Wide Web at: USPS.GOV. Visit the Web site to download information. Doing so is very easy if your computer has the Adobe's Acrobat Reader application (.PDF file extensions.) If not, go to the Web site FTPSEARCH.COM and download the ar32e301.exe file; double-click it when it is in the correct drive and the problem is solved, all for free. For example, USPS has a number of Quick Service Guides on the Web: 630 to 633, 640 to 644, and 670. All these guides are published in one publication, No. 95 (August 1997). Publication 417, from October 1996, details nonprofit standard mail eligibility: *Nonprofit and Other Qualified Organizations*. These publications and many others are obtainable from local Postal Business Centers or by writing USPS, 475 L'Enfant Plaza SW, Washington, D.C. 20260-2405. Some of these centers also sponsor free Bulk Mail Seminars.

If a mailing is over 200 pieces, a nonprofit may want to investigate bulk mailing, as rates for nonprofits can be substantially lower than first-class mail. But, due to initial costs of $85 for the annual fee and $85 as a one-time indicia fee, a mailing has to be approximately 1,000 pieces to break even. Since rates and regulations change frequently (a change is to be made in January 1999), check with the local post office for the latest information. At current rates, a first class stamp costs 32 cents and nonprofit bulk mail rate is 13.2 cents.

Consider using a reliable commercial mail house if regular mailings are over 500 pieces; doing so might save a lot of anguish and staff and volunteer time.

Now let us discuss the first-class way of handling mail. If funds are available, always mail the formal invitation and the event committee invitation letter first class. There are two reasons: First, it is the most economical way to clean up your address list. If the address is incorrect, the mailed item will be returned with a correct address (if the recipient left a forwarding address). Second, when asking people to join a committee to raise money and/or to contribute money, it is always classier to have the request arrive first class. Save-the-date cards and letters can be bulk mailed if and only if they are mailed in ample time to *arrive* the scheduled number of weeks prior to the event (at least 20 weeks before, which means that the bulk mail must be at the post office 23 weeks prior to the event). (See the METT.)

INSURANCE

Most organizations have a general liability insurance policy; if an agency does not, contact an insurance broker immediately. Special events are covered by purchasing a rider for a specific event. A rider is an additional policy that covers liability situations for the specific event—for example, accidents such as a guest tripping on the dance floor and breaking an arm or a leg, bursting water pipes that soak and ruin guests' clothing, and, perish the thought, food poisoning. Then there is a very special type of insurance: the Hole-in-One insurance policy for golf tournaments. This type of policy allows an organization to offer a large monetary prize for a hole-in-one at a very low cost. Of course, special conditions must be met; these are spelled out in the policy. If agencies love to host golf tournaments, they should purchase this type of policy.

If the special event is an auction or an art show, the rider will protect the nonprofit against theft and defacement of the artwork. Insurance companies provide a list of guidelines to follow to protect their and an agency's interests, should the organization be fortunate enough to have a famous art piece to auction. Insurance companies lose money if they pay a loss—therefore, they want to protect everyone's interests.

Is there an insurance company that specializes in writing policies for nonprofits? Yes, at least in California: Nonprofits' Insurance Alliance of California (NIAC) provides complete insurance coverage for California 501(c)(3) IRS designated nonprofits. This is not an endorsement. However, NIAC publishes a booklet on what safety features to look for when an event is produced. This publication covers the entire special event process, from appointing a safety czar to legal considerations if an accident happens (including sample forms needed). Usually NIAC will mail one copy to a nonprofit even if an agency is not a policyholder. (See Resource Section for their address.)

Is there an insurance broker on the board of directors? If so, approach him or her about this special coverage. A broker who is a member of the board might refer the agency to another brokerage house so as to avoid writing a policy where he or she receives a commission. The other board members might resent using one company over another; it is always best to use a board non-affiliated company. Professional staff must approach this matter with great delicacy; they do not want to offend an active board member, nor do they want to fail to seek out expert assistance from someone who would keep the agency's interests in mind and could steer the nonprofit away from dangerous and expensive commitments. Check with the board president or the chair of the executive committee and adhere to their advise.

PRINTING AND PRINTERS

If an organization is located in or near a metropolitan area, investigate the possibility of using a print broker. Large printers must keep their presses rolling 24 hours a day, 365 days a year, in order to be competitive and make a profit. They employ brokers to bring in business during the slack hours; the business helps pay the craftspeople's wages, which in turn helps nonprofits get very good prices on their printing requirements.

When requesting a quotation from a printer, be prepared to provide the following information:

- Quantity of printed piece and its parts; for example, must a return card and envelope be enclosed?
- Size of each piece
- Type of paper—coated or plain—and the quality and weight of the paper stock
- Black and white or color (multicolor or just one?)
- Person responsible for designing the piece and preparing the copy for the printer
- Delivery date

Nonprofits generally use two sizes for invitations: A6 and A7. A6 measures four by six inches; A7, seven by five inches. The paper used for invitations can be cut to form four- or six-panel configurations. Many types of paper can be used; however, the usual types are 80# coated gloss cover, matte coated, or uncoated. As an example, an A7, four-panel, 80#-coated gloss cover, with an outer envelope and a translucent paper insert plus a return card and envelope will weigh just one ounce and can be mailed for 32 cents. Many organizations design their own invitations and other marketing pieces using computer software. Material must be provided in digital format; Macintosh computers specialize in this; however, PC users can employ Adobe Pro Publishing applications for similar results.

Invitations are one of an organization's up-front marketing pieces, and many go overboard with design and color, die-cut shapes, and overweight invitation packages. Make sure that the cost of the marketing goodies do not exceed the funds the event raises for the agency.

It is a good marketing idea to select a specific design for each event. For example, Dinner à la Heart could have a heart as its symbol, either a solid one in black and white or a red one if funds permit. A graphic artist could produce a specially designed heart; the main point is to have the heart symbol on every piece of paper (including envelopes) printed for the event. Chapter 6 provides a complete discussion of symbols, logos, and marketing efforts.

Earlier chapters mentioned the ad journal (or program book). Whatever it is called, this attractive marketing piece can produce a large amount of revenue—often 10 percent of the funds raised—at a reasonable cost. A nonprofit can insert graphics and text highlighting its history, current programs, and plans for the future in the journal's marketing text. Various types of advertisements appear, generally offering congratulations to the honoree and/or the nonprofit. Corporate ads should not be overtly commercial; many corporations feature only their logo in an ad. Many individuals who cannot attend the event but want to support the nonprofit or thank the honoree for their community involvement, or both, take out advertisements expressing their good wishes.

The design used for the invitation also can be used for the ad journal. A good size for this book is 8½ by 11 inches with a landscape (horizontal) layout so when looking at the book, each page is approximately 8½ inches high and 5½ inches in width. This makes four pages per folded-over sheet, and a mock up can be made easily. (Plan the book in units of four pages.) In fact, if there is a computer genius on the nonprofit's staff, then sample pages can be produced and used by committee members to obtain commitments from the people and organizations they contact. Organizations usually provide camera-ready copy. Individuals usually provide text they want on the ad and leave it up to the nonprofit to produce the camera-ready copy for the printer. There is no extra charge for text ads, but a charge should be made for intricate non-camera ready copy that includes graphics. (Many times this is a negotiable item.)

What is the ad journal going to cost? And will sales produce a profit? The price of these books varies in every location, but a *rule-of-thumb* calculation would be between $5 and $12 per copy to print. If an event is going to draw 500 guests, the cost will vary between $2,500 and $6,000. (Adjust this cost for printing 80 percent of 500 copies: $2,000 to $4,800.) Why print 80 percent of the anticipated attendance? Because unfortunately, not everyone who planned to attend the event will show up, and only 70 to 80 percent will take a copy home with them even though it is free! If an event is going to be the exception, print 100 percent of estimated attendance, a profit will still be made. How? Look again at Exhibit 3.2, Tribute Event Pricing. Using the high figure of $6,000 and if only good-wishes ads are sold, then 40 such ads at $150 will bring in $6,000. Realistically, this will not happen. Committee members will sell a full range of ads in the black-and-white category; if the event is properly marketed, they will also sell a few gold and silver pages. A profit will be evident before the deadline arrives.

ADDITIONAL CONSIDERATIONS: DECORATIONS, ENTERTAINMENT, AND FEEDING THE VOLUNTEERS

Decoration of the event site should be a consideration in choosing one venue over another. For example, if your event features a circus theme and the agency wants to "redecorate" the main ballroom and even bring in animals, the availability of sites can be restricted—there may be only one or two to choose from in your community.

Special entertainment beyond the usual dance band or string trio brought in to provide background music can also be a factor in the selection of a site. If your plan calls for a rock concert, you are probably going to have to select the largest auditorium in the community. You may need to arrange to hold it outdoors, which requires permits from the city or county and the governing police force. This in turn brings up the subject of security. Some agencies must arrange for special security because of their special mission in the community, which brings out local pickets and/or unknown potential problems. In addition, if your guest keynote speaker is a prominent national or international personality or celebrity, then the agency has to provide security. Security can be arranged through the hiring of off duty local police or sheriff deputies, or from private security agencies that provide trained licensed personnel.

Finally, if you are hiring extra people or have an extraordinary number of volunteers, plan to feed them. This can be accomplished in one of two ways: either have them fill-in at tables that have empty seats because of no shows (after all the agency has guaranteed a certain number of dinners, and it is a shame to pay for food that is not consumed) or, in your planning with the catering manager, have a separate section set up for the support staff, security people, and others that will be assisting at the event, but will not be taking part in it.

ADDITIONAL ADMINISTRATIVE CONCERNS

Besides the decoration of the site, there are other considerations the special event professional must look at to achieve success. The site you choose might have all the facilities required to produce the event, but it might have policies that discriminate against one class of citizen because of race, religion, or ethnic origin. Yes, it's almost the beginning of the 21st century, but some venues are private and some do discriminate. The nonprofit must look at a situation like this and take the high road, the only road, and change the venue.

Throughout the United States there are agencies (Meals on Wheels, for example) that feed the poor and sick and are financed through donations of money and most importantly food! If your agency holds a reception and at the end find that you have a lot of food left over, donate it to the agnecy in your community. Make arrangements for this donation beforehand, so that the food can be disttributed immediately, while it is fresh. Does your agency want to receive brownie points in the form of PR exposure for this act of generosity? A meeting of the minds, between the agency professional, board president, and event chair, should be held to discuss the pros and cons of tooting the agency's horn. In many instances, the recipient agency will automatically make some kind of acknowledgment to the public, especially when the donation becomes a regular act; in this way, the recipient agency also motivates other groups to emulate your agency.

A note about Exhibit 7.4, the catering contract. It purposely shows the reader a unique document, rather than the usual hotel catering contract. Both cover the same details, but of course in different formats. As

METT Checklist for Chapter 7

Week	To Do This Week	Book Ref.	☑
6	Catering negotiations begin; prepare and mail catering specifications to selected vendors; if location has already been selected, discuss specifications with catering manager. Check insurance requirements and determine if special governmental permits are required.		
7	Select printer and mailing house; check postage rates; work with graphic designer on invitation layout.		

with all contracts, if the agency is unsure about the terms, have the agency's attorney look at it and advise you if everything is as it should be, without any traps that your agency cannot live with.

FINANCIAL MATTERS

Most events are prepaid affairs—guests send their checks to the agency prior to attending or the agency invoices them immediately after the event. Sometimes guests bring checks and even cash to the event. No matter how the money is received, always stamp the checks with the agency's deposit stamp and deposit the checks (and cash) immediately. This promptness will lessen the chance of receiving a "not-sufficient-funds" notice from the bank. Always pay vendors as contracted; the agency's reputation demands this courtesy to those suppliers who have given the organization good quality and service at an agreed-upon price. Information about payment delays has a way of seeping out into the community; the next time an event is planned, it will be harder to obtain good prices and terms.

In most agencies, the above details are handled by the nonprofit's accountant or bookkeeper. Many times the development staff receives the checks prior to the accounting department, so that they can record the payment for their records. No matter what system is used, procedures have to be established and followed so that the accounting for the money received tallies in both departments.

Also remember the board of directors and event chairs; if they have arranged good prices and terms with some vendors and then receive a telephone call about payment, not only is the agency's reputation in the gutter, but volunteers will not be so eager to work with the agency again.

CONCLUSION

Administration is the process where all the i's are dotted and the t's are crossed. However special events administration also delves into common sense and unique areas. The agency's professional staff usually handles administrative matters for special events. Chapter 8 features a drop-dead checklist and time line (a subset of the METT) where these administrative items will again be pushed into the foreground.

CHAPTER EIGHT

The Final Weeks to Event Day

MASTER EVENT TIMETABLE INTRODUCTION

The Master Event Timetable (METT) tells us that when week 18 begins, it is the final push to week 26: event day. The agency must accomplish four tasks by event day so that all the details that make a successful event compared to an ordinary one are taken care of.

The first task involves motivation techniques that can be used with the event chairs, committee members, and all of the volunteers so that they are encouraged to finish their job(s) of soliciting gifts in the form of in-kind items, donations, sponsorships or underwriting of major segments of the event, advertisements for the program journal, and the purchase of tables and individual seats.

The second task, one that can be very frustrating and is in itself an artform, is the seating of guests at an event. Seating arrangements are of concern mainly at testimonial and award events and others where a sit-down meal is provided. This chapter discusses in detail the science and art of seating guests. Since where people sit is very important to them, it is extremely important to the nonprofit.

The third task in producing the event is the preparation of the documents that form the communication links so that everyone involved with the project—both volunteers and professional staff—knows what to do, when and where to do it, and who is responsible for their segment of the event. The documents include time lines, checklists, agendas, and scripts.

The fourth task is the completion of Exhibit 8.5, the PDQ Checklist, which is to used in conjunction with the METT. PDQ stands for people, documents, and queries. When both of these documents are followed in tandem, there emerges a blueprint that the event staff and volunteers can follow until the big day arrives.

MOTIVATIONAL TECHNIQUES FOR EVENT COMMITTEE MEMBERS

As mentioned, the one and only committee meeting is held during week 14. During week 15 the committee members receive their first copy of the weekly event reservation log, which shows them the status of the event as of the previous Friday. By viewing this log, which lists how many people have purchased seats, tables, advertisements, and made donations, committee members begin to grasp the complete picture of the event. This log is a prime motivational technique because it allows everyone involved with the event to chart its progress. It is a basic communication marketing technique. Marketing is not confined to just the public; the agency's staff also need to be enthusiastic about the work of the entire nonprofit, and communication of what the agency has accomplished now, by producing a special event. Use the marketing plan outlined in Chapter 6 as a motivational strategy for the event committee members and the in-house volunteers and staff.

The following scenario can be used to motivate the prominent committee members. This peer-to-peer method aims to involve these very busy people in an agency's program by asking them to contact their peers and solicit their assistance in supporting the event. This plan is especially good for those prominent corporate types who do not attend the committee meeting or do not submit a list of names promptly. They have agreed to serve on the committee; do not let their initial enthusiasm dry up. By following this scenario, the event chair has a better than even chance to give interested but uninvolved committee members meaningful assignments.

THE HOT-PROSPECT SCENARIO

Immediately after the event committee meeting, the chair, co-chairs, and agency professional staff compare the name lists sent by committee members to the nonprofit against the master list. The screening accomplishes two main goals: One, it checks for duplications, especially among the larger prospects; the event chair does not want hot prospects to be approached independently by two different committee members, although it is OK to approach non-hot prospects twice. Second, the event chair makes sure the hot prospect is approached by the peer committee member he or she cannot say no to. For example, the chief executive officer of the largest bank in the community should be approached by the CEO of the bank's largest customer; the next choice would be to have the CEO from one of the largest firms in the area contact this person. Contact people with an account at the bank will be of some help; however, a contact person currently unaffiliated with the bank would be even better for the event, as the event will serve as a vehicle for the banker to get closer to a potential customer in a friendly and natural manner, when they are both doing public service. The main motivational push begins in week 20 and 21, when the event chair and co-chairs start evaluating how many prospective table buyers and advertisers have responded. The event chair and co-chairs split up the responsibility of contacting the committee members who have outstanding prospects who need some nudging to make their commitments. Depending on how many prospective names are on the combined master and committee member list, usually event chairs need help in contacting prospective attendees. When these prospects (usually the ones who are classified by the committee to purchase less than a table) appear on the prospect screen, it is incumbent upon the agency's professional staff to make the follow-up contact in the name of one of the event chairs; Exhibit 8.1 (CH0801.DOC) is a short telephone script that can be used for this follow-up call.

MOTIVATION TECHNIQUES FOR COMMITTEE MEMBERS!

During these follow-up weeks, an agency can use many motivational programs to spur on the event committee members. These include a weekly contest for the committee member who books the greatest number of reservations and one for the member who brings in the largest number of advertisements. Prizes could be an event T-shirt or a Cross ballpoint pen with the agency's logo on the clip. When the list of committee members is finalized, way back in weeks 14 and 15, an added motivational goodie is a special business card with the name of the committee member and all of the event information on it. Scratch pads and Post-it Notes also can be used as motivational freebees: No matter

Exhibit 8.1   Telephone Scripts for Event Committee Members

"Hello [cheerfully] my name is _____ . I am calling for Mr./Mrs./Ms. _____ , the chair of the (name of agency) annual award dinner. This is a follow-up call to make sure you received the letter (name of event chair) mailed to you on (approximate date). Can I help you by answering any questions concerning the dinner?"
  [State the following, whichever is applicable:]
      A. "Our records show that you (and/or your firm) attended this event in the past (or last year)."
      B. "Thank you for your past support!"
      C. "I understand that you have never attended one of our award events." [Briefly describe the event and what will take place that evening or at the auction, tournament, etc.] [At this point you should have a hint of what the prospect is planning to do, if anything. If the conversation has been comfortable—if the prospect was interested in talking about the event, then suggest that a commitment be made:]
      1. Number of reservations
      2. An advertisement
      3. A gift (if the prospects say they are unavailable on the date of the event).
  ALL RESPONSES, POSITIVE, OR I'LL GET BACK TO YOU, OR NEGATIVE MUST BE ACKNOWLEDGED WITH:
          "Thank you for your time" and "I will send the information
          you requested in today's mail [fax, or e-mail]" or
              "When can I telephone you again?"

how prestigious a committee, everyone likes to see his name in print and personalized on items that can be used to communicate to prospects. Almost every software publishing program has some sort of business card template; the card blanks are available at office supply stores at very reasonable prices.

Make sure each committee member has a copy of the Seven Goals for a Successful Special Event. Use the one in the Introduction, or customize it for the particular event. The inherent nature of fund raising makes it a money-oriented program; however, the other six goals will benefit the nonprofit and at the same time make the special event a complete program that volunteers can participate in and be proud of; only jaded volunteers will not respond to a multilevel program that benefits their nonprofit.

Remember these key words throughout the event committee process and the motivational program: excite, stimulate, influence, and communicate! Fun it up! (Don't dumb it down.)

SEATING GUESTS

Guests will remember the event for many of the goals it achieves and what they learn about the agency; but one item will always stick in guests' minds: where they sat in relation to the center of activities and to the head table, and how compatible they were with the people at their table (if they only purchased one or two tickets, instead of a full table). Three types of guests purchase a few tickets instead of a table: the nonprofit's largest supporters who give four- or five-figure gifts also support the event by purchasing a few tickets (although some major supporters are generous to a fault and also purchase a full table); annual supporters who like to attend the event to socialize with casual acquaintances and also support the agency; and the first-time event guests (mainly the newly recruited event committee members). All of these people have to be made welcome and seated as if they were as important as the full-table purchasers—which they are! By the way, these guests know they will not be seated at the "best" table; they just do not want to be in Siberia. At this point the art of seating takes over from the science.

Whether using software designed for special events or a do-it-yourself database described in Chapter 3 (Exhibit 3.6), information about guest reservations is entered into fields in the database program. Fields have been provided for the names of the guests attending, table number and table name, either for full tables or partial reservations. Thus one entry allows the agency to record the number of guest reservations, their names, entrée preferences, if they purchased an advertisement, and if they want to be seated with friends; all this pertinent information is necessary to keep track of how the event is progressing.

To make life simple, assign a table number immediately when a reservation is made, whether for a full table or for a partial one. (When reservations come in ones and twos, just place the first ten guests at one table and the next ten at another.) On the day the number-of-guests-attending guarantee is made, sketch out the table design arrangement on the floor schematic the catering manager provided. Number each table, starting with 1, the table of honor; then place the tables around that table in a concentric oval, until the required number is reached. (Depending on the number of people who will sit at the table of honor, it can be either a large oval table or a series of tables of ten; if the latter is the case, number them 1, 2, 3, etc.)

After numbering the tables, name them. Name full tables after the purchaser's business or corporation or some other appropriate name; name partial tables after the organization that purchased the most seats, or an individual who did so. If the agency has many programs with unique names, those can be used for table names: Be creative! Why use table names? Doing so gives the nonprofit another opportunity to thank supporters by using their corporate name or logo on the table signpost with the number. It is good marketing for the agency and it lets every-one see that Big Shot Incorporated purchased a table, which makes them feel very good, especially if the senior management is attending the event. The next time the agency holds an event, those people will remember the good treatment they received at its last function.

RECEPTION AND CHECK-IN DESK

The reception area and check-in desk is located where all who are attending must walk by. Check-in areas are necessary to ensure that only people who have paid actually attend the event; those guests who have not paid can do so at check-in time. By having guests check in, the event staff can keep a count of the number of guests attending at each table. The person in charge of the event needs this information to keep the room from looking unbalanced. Occasionally an entire table of a sponsoring group might not attend, and an empty table in the section near the table of honor would look very much out of place. Sometimes this information is not conveyed to the agency until the very last minute, or the tables sponsor tells a friend who is attending the event that they are not coming, hence, the news is not learned until the friend arrives. By keeping a count of the guests who have arrived and their table numbers, staff will have enough time to renumber the tables or to move one off the floor.

Prior to the guests' arrival, agency staff and volunteers lay out table cards (Exhibit 8.2, ▊CH0802.DOC) on the reception desk. These cards list the name of the guest(s) and the table number, and are arranged in alphabetical order. Also, copies of the table chart and Alpha Seating Chart (Exhibits 8.3 and 8.4, ▊CH0803.DOC and CH0804.DOC) are available for double-checking if there is a question about seating or meal choice. Both of these exhibits are essentially the same with the information placed in different formats: The Table Chart shows the guests seated at each table, sorted by table number and name; the Alpha Seating Chart lists all guests alphabetically by last name, and includes their table number and any special food requirements. The catering manager and the room captain also should receive copies of both these charts, so that they know where special meals will be served. Remember: Anything the agency's staff and volunteers can do to make the serving of food easier will result in a smoother and more successful event. Sometimes placing a large schematic of the dining area with all the tables numbered and named on an easel at the entrance to the dining room makes it easier for guests to locate their table.

The volunteer or staff person in charge of the reception desk should have all of the items needed to run a small office: pens, pencils, staples, scissors, highlight marker pens, poster board for last-minute signs

Exhibit 8.2 Sample Table Card

NONPROFIT'S LOGO
Mr. & Mrs. Donald Generous Donor
You are seated at table 1.

Exhibit 8.3 Table Chart

Name of Guest	Table No.	Table Name	No. of Seats	Fish	Beef	Veggies
Alpha Charity Dinner **May 31, 1998**						
Geo. Washington	1	VIP'ers	1	X		
Tom Jefferson	1		1		X	
Winston Churchill	1		1	X		
Franklin Roosevelt	1		1			X
Eleanor Roosevelt	1		1	X		
Golda Meir	1		1			X
Martha Cooley	1		1	X		
Lyllian Wendroff	1		1	X		
Marion Anderson	1		1			X
Joh. Brahms	1		1		X	
TOTALS:	10		10	5	2	3

Exhibit 8.4   Alpha Chart

	A	B	C	D	E	F	G	H	I
1	FNAME	LNAME			TABLE #	COMMENT			
2	Jim	Armstrong			1	VIP PLACE.			
3	Jimmy	Carter			1	VIP PLACE.			
4	Bill	Clinton			4	Veg. Plate			
5	Janet	Reno			8	VIP PLACE.			
6	Alan	Wendroff			10	KOSHER			
7	Lillian	Wendroff			2	Special Seating			
8									
9									
10									
11									
12									
13									
14									
15									
16									
17									
18									
19									
20									
21									
22									
23									
24									
25									
26									
27									
28									
29									
30									

(especially if the agency is displaying program material), a first-aid kit, and computer items if a laptop computer will be used.

DOCUMENTS

Many documents are needed for the event, including the PDQ Checklist, reservation log (only for event chair(s)), table and alpha charts for seating guests, schematic drawing of the event room or site, and lists of people who will be attending (besides the guests) who should be greeted and thanked personally by one of the chairs or agency board members. (Such people include event committee members, ad journal purchasers, media representatives, VIPs, and honorary chairs.) Other necessary documents include lists of people who must be photographed, the event day time line, and script(s) for the program and, if necessary, the audio/video presentation. These documents make up what is referred to as the Complete Set of Event Day documents; they should be bound in a soft-cover folder.

The following documents are assembled for each event:

1. Event day time line
2. Event program timed script
3. Schematic drawing of event site, indicating placement of guest tables, table(s) of honor, podium, dance floor, reception area, and nonprofit's program booth(s)
4. Alpha list of all guests, indicating seating arrangements and special requirements
5. Table list of all guests (a list of tables indicating who is sitting there)
6. VIP list, e.g., celebrities, politicians, and major givers
7. Photographer's list, e.g., photographs that must be taken at the event, e.g., the honoree with the guest speaker, etc.
8. PDQ checklist
9. Award citation printed in large (14–18 pt.) type

Because the time line for the day of the event is so important, Chapter 9 is written in a time-line format, starting at 9 A.M. of the event day (if the event is an all-day affair, such as a golf tournament, the time line would start the day before) and ending when the event is scheduled to conclude, around 9:30 P.M. or later if the event is a dinner dance. When an evening event is scheduled to begin at 6:30 P.M., there will be a time line within a time line. The more detailed time line, known as the event program time line, is the one used by the event chairs, emcees, the catering department, and professional staff. This minute-by-minute time line lists specific details on what everyone does during the crucial time between the opening reception and the benediction or closing remarks.

Special Event Tip

If dancing is part of the event, then how long the event lasts after the close of the formal program is a function of how long the guests want to dance. This is the fun time of the event, and guests should be allowed to linger. If the orchestra has been engaged for a specific time, extending that time by an hour might be a good idea. It is a good marketing strategy, for guests who have a good time will remember the event and the nonprofit.

In the packet along with the event program time line is a bulleted script for the event's program. Most volunteers are grateful to receive information on just what the nonprofit wants them to say. A professional staff member should write a simple script for volunteers who have to introduce people and make special announcements; the emcee and guest speaker will prepare their own comments. (The emcee also needs a copy of the event program time line so that he or she can make appropriate comments at the correct time and a list of the VIPs in attendance so that they can be introduced at the proper time.) A volunteer must keep track of the VIPs: whether they show up and where they are sitting. The volunteer must keep the emcee informed of these details; introduce the VIP volunteer to the emcee as soon as they both check in for the event. This volunteer also can assist the photographer by pointing out the VIPs so that photographs can be taken with the honoree, event chair, agency board president, and so on. A photo list should be drawn up in advance.

The script also should list the exact wording of the award that is presented to the honoree. Often the engraving on such awards is difficult to read; there is nothing more embarrassing for the award presenter than to have to stumble over the inscription when giving the award to the honoree.

SETTING THE PACE FOR THE EVENT

Throughout the formal program, from the reception to the ending benediction, the staff professional in charge is the one to give the signal to dim the lights and start moving the guests from the reception to the dining room. (Recruit volunteers to assist in this task, preferably very tall, outgoing people who can break in on guests' conversations to remind them about dinner.) This staff person must start the formal program on time and set the pace for the remainder of the event. The staff person in charge is the "pusher" who reminds the emcee and speakers prior to their appearance.

THE PDQ CHECKLIST

The checklist seen in Exhibit 8.5 (CH0805.DOC) is the peace-of-mind checklist; it covers all of the items that must be double- and triple-checked to make sure the event will be successful.

As mentioned, PDQ means people, documents, and queries. The checklist is divided into these three logical categories.

People

This category lists everyone involved during the final weeks leading to the event day and those who will be an integral part of the event day. Names and office and cellular telephone numbers are required. All these people will receive the Event Program Time Line (see Chapter 9) plus other particular documents (listed in the Comments column) relating to their unique activity at the event. Why does the event chair or staff member speak to every person on this list before the event? First, if the person has a special responsibility at the event—say, to introduce a guest speaker—it is a way to make sure the staff professional and the volunteer are on the same wavelength. Second, if the volunteer has no specific duty at the event other than to be the nonprofit's spokesperson at the table, the nonprofit professional wants to make sure that the person actually will attend and is motivated to talk about the agency in general and perhaps about a special program in particular. Ideally, all event co-chairs, honorary chairs, and event committee members should be assigned a job to carry out at the event. Not all will attend; illness, business trips, and family responsibilities will keep some of these people away. Nevertheless, those who do attend have been working for the event and the nonprofit for many months and are the best people to explain the agency to the other guests.

Documents

This category of the checklist indicates all the documents that must be completed and on hand for the event day; included are the event day checklist, time lines, agendas, scripts, the award plaque inscription, seating charts, volunteer lists, permits, and licenses, among others.

Queries

Queries are the "has this been done" items that must be completed to make the event successful. For example, have the reception and check-in tables been set up at the entrance to the event site? Has the in-kind donation of wine arrived and been unloaded at the event site? Does the photographer know whom to photograph by sight? (Have a volunteer introduce the photographer to the people in question.)

Tip

If this event is large, both in number of potential guests and scope of activities, buy, rent, or borrow a cellular telephone and a beeper at least five to

Exhibit 8.5   The PDQ Checklist

Category	Comments & Notes	☑
PEOPLE⇓⇓		
Event chair	Name & Telephone No(s). + necessary documents	
Event co-chair/ad journal	List of Ad buyers and table numbers	
Event co-chair/event committee	List of committee members attending	
Event co-chair/marketing and PR	List of media people attending	
Event co-chair/catering and site	Alpha & Table list; catering instructions and table schematic	
Honorary chairs	Event Program Time Line	
Agency president	Complete set of Event Day Documents	
Guest speaker(s)	Event Program Time Line	
Rabbi/Priest/Pastor	Event Program Time Line	
Emcee	Event Program Time Line + VIP list	
Entertainer(s)	Event Program Time Line	
Photographer	Event Program Time Line + special whom-to-photograph list	
Volunteer coordinator	Event Program Time Line + list of volunteers and assignments + Exhibits 4.5 & 4.6	
Catering manager	Event Program Time Line + table list w/special requests for each table and table schematic	
Food and beverage director	Event Program Time Line	
Agency executive director	Complete set of all documents	
Agency professional staff	Event Program Time Line	
Agency support staff	Event Program Time Line	
Volunteer VIP person	Event Program Time Line + list of VIPs and honorary chairs	
Volunteer audio/video person	Event Program Time Line + Scripts for special presentations	
DOCUMENTS⇓⇓	THE COMPLETE SET OF EVENT DAY DOCUMENTS⇓	
Event reservation log		
Alpha list of guests		
Table list of guests		
Room table schematic		

Exhibit 8.5 *(continued)*

Category	Comments & Notes	☑
List of attending event committee members		
List of ad journal buyers with table numbers		
List of attending media representatives		
List of VIPs and honorary chairs		
Photographer's list		
Event Program Time Line		
Event program script		
Audio and video scripts for special presentations		
QUERY⇓⇓		
Set up registration area	Accomplish two hours before start of event	
Oversee audio/video presentation	Rehearsal four hours prior to the start of event	
Check dining room table layout and number	With catering manager and/or banquet captain one hour prior to the start of the event	
Set up display areas for nonprofit's programmatic presentations	Three to four hours prior to the start of the event	
Monitor receipt and distribution of in-kind donations	Check with donors/event site first thing in the morning of the event	
Distribute nonprofit's marketing material at each table	Finish at least one hour prior to the start of the event	
Check to make sure the awards are at the podium (unwrapped)	One hour prior to the start of the event	

seven days prior to the event day. Also, *never* be without the PDQ Checklist during this time; keep it at your bedside for those last-minute calls.

Another Tip

Make sure that everyone who is making decisions about the event has a copy of the PDQ Checklist. As with most endeavors, communication is a prime asset!

The PDQ Checklist works this way: Beside each title in the People category, place the name of the person(s) responsible and their telephone number(s): office, home, pager, and cellular/mobile, plus, if required, a special comment. In the Document category, note down how many must be on hand at the site and who receives them, then place a red check mark on the right-hand side of the checklist. In the Queries section, which outlines specific projects that must be done before the event begins and those that take place during the program, put the names of the people responsible for each task in the comments section and a red check mark it when it is completed.

Exhibit 8.5 is not a complete listing for an event, just a sample. The event each nonprofit produces will use some of these descriptions and add others that are unique. For example, auctions and tournaments require exacting details in order to be successful; community-wide events, such as a 10K run/walk, must be thought out ahead of time. Since they require many volunteers, they require a master PDQ Checklist that is divided into subsections so that each segment of the event is accomplished correctly and on time.

Remember, never be stingy! It is better to list more detail than less. Why? Because, when the checklist is completed, the potential problems will have been resolved and all the staff and volunteers involved will have been briefed and on the same page.

METT Checklist for Chapter 8

Week	To Do This Week	Book Ref.	☑
18	Begin motivation of committee members; accomplished by event chair(s) and professional staff		
to 23			
24	Start writing and assembling documents for event day.		
25	Complete PDQ checklist and implement tasks.		
26	EVENT DAY—All duties are explained in Chapter 9.		

CONCLUSION

This chapter takes the planning of the event from week 18 to the actual event day. Combining the METT with the PDQ Checklist, there is a step-by-step progression starting with the motivation factors that can be used to encourage event committee members to complete their tasks, through the art of seating the guests, then to the preparation of the necessary documentation that will make the event run smoothly, to the PDQ checklist, which will nail down all the to dos. All of this information should be placed in a three-ring binder divided into the four key elements: goals, planning, organization, and administration.

CHAPTER NINE

The Big Day: Why the Success Is in the Details

INTRODUCTION

As mentioned previously, special events are detailed oriented. Why? Whether the event is a testimonial dinner, a major gift parlor meeting or reception, a golf tournament, or an auction, the prospective givers come to the nonprofit. No other fund-raising program has this advantage. Consider the direct mail letter. If readers get by the first sentence of the first paragraph, it is considered a success. (Some pundits feel that if the envelope is opened it is a miracle.) What are the odds of being hung up on while making a telephone solicitation to an unknown prospect: 500 to 1? But, for a special event, these same people are getting into their automobiles and traveling some distance, many times paying an arm and a leg for parking. Most important, they have donated more money than they ever thought they would to your nonprofit. In return, they receive dinner or lunch or hors d'oeuvres, a glass of wine, and a program of indeterminate length and interest. And this is why the details are important. The event must flow smoothly. All the elements must mesh together and be combined with a large dollop of creativity to produce an interesting program that will place the agency in the spotlight so it can achieve the seven goals for a successful special event.

A word about creativity. Know the audience; for example, if the event is for attorneys, obtain a guest speaker who will appeal to the audience but also has a reputation in his or her field and is an interesting speaker. Many times, prominent people with national reputations and followings bore everyone. Such a situation will not reflect well on the agency the next time it plans a special event. Again, attention to details in researching possible speakers or entertainers will result in an interesting event that will be remembered.

Do not waste the unique opportunity to impress prospects on the agency's own turf by failing to plan properly. Impress guests at the event in a few of the following ways:

- Have an exceptional presentation at the nonprofit's program booth.
- Have a quality speaker discuss the agency during the formal program.
- Distribute high-quality printed material at the table or in the information kit given to each participant.
- Have a knowledgeable agency spokesperson sit at each table or be a part of each golf foursome.
- Provide a meaningful give-a-way item for each guest.

To impress guests, the five points listed above have to be accomplished in a manner that draws attention to the work of your agency. For example, the presentation at the program booth cannot just be a table with brochures and posters scattered around; it is imperative that the program managers be in attendance when your agency sets up a booth at the event. Make the printed information readable and attractive through the use of photos, large type, and a size that is easy to take home—a vest-pocket-size brochure is an excellent choice. Also, in this era of high tech computer equipment, an audio/video presentation is an inexpensive way to promote the agency's work. Ask a local corporation's MIS department to assist the agency by donating this type of technical assistance. In addition, a videotape presentation can be produced and presented at the booth without a great amount of expense or trouble.

THE FINAL COUNTDOWN

When combined with the PDQ Checklist, the Event Day Time Line will place everyone on the right path toward a successful special event. This event example begins at 6:30 P.M. and formally concludes at 9:30 P.M. Exhibit 9.1 (CH0901.DOC)

Exhibit 9.2 (CH0902.DOC) is the time line that applies to the actual event. When the guests arrive for the reception until they leave after the dinner and program, is the most crucial time of the event. Your guests will not tolerate a slow, boring, and drawn-out testimonial event. If they want to remain after the program is over, so they can dance or talk to friends they only see at events like this, then that is their choice; they do not want to be embarrassed and conspicuous by leaving the ballroom before the program ends. It is the professional's job to keep the program on time. The best way to do this is to have it start on time. Do not let the program wait until the guests have their second cup of coffee; in fact, the program after dinner can begin when the desserts have been served, but not completely eaten. The professional and the emcee must be in agreement with the timing issue, otherwise the event can be a disaster!

EVENT DAY—TIME LINE

Combined with the PDQ Checklist, Exhibit 8.5, this time line for Event Day will place the volunteers and professional staff on the same page, informationally speaking. It cannot be stressed too often: Communication is the main key to producing a successful special event that achieves the seven goals—both are programmatic and administrative—explained in detail in the Introduction and Chapter 1. This chapter, and especially this time line, concentrates on the logistical part of the event. In addition, the degree of perfection of the special event will show the guests that future support of the agency is worthwhile because if the staff can produce a "smashing" event they can also run their programs in the same efficient way.

Exhibit 9.1   Event Schedule: An Example

9:00 A.M.	Nonprofit professional reads through PDQ Checklist (Exhibit 8.5) to make sure all items are checked. (If the event starts in the morning or at noon, read through the PDQ the night before.)
9:30	Nonprofit professional checks mail, faxes, and e-mail for last-minute reservations.
10:00	Telephone event chair(s) and those committee members who have been very responsive to the event for last-minute changes and reservations. Agency support staff or volunteers telephone full-table purchasers for the names of their guests (if necessary). Check receipt of in-kind gifts.
11:00	Meet with support staff and volunteers who will be assisting at the event and make sure everyone knows his or her role and has the backup documents and information to proceed. Agency staff should check the following: 1. Reconcile the reservation log with the alpha seating and table charts to make sure the guest numbers are correct; if in doubt, go through the guests' individual reservation cards to make sure they are inputted in the log and charts. 2. The person in charge of reservation desk at the event must make sure the following items are ready to be taken to the event site: 　a. Individual table cards (Exhibit 8.2) with blank extras 　b. Name tags and ribbons (if applicable) 　c. All documents: program journals, scripts, time lines, charts, agency brochures, reservation log, alpha and table charts; have 5 extra sets available for those people who forgot to bring theirs 　d. Laptop computer and printer (if applicable) 　e. Small metal box (with key) for checks and cash 　f. Special handouts or table literature from sponsoring corporations 　g. Pens, pencils, paper clips, and staples
Noon	If necessary, speak with catering manager about guest guarantee number. Ascertain whereabouts of out-of-town speakers and special guests.
12:30 to 2:00 P.M.	Have a relaxing lunch at a favorite restaurant. (If all documentation has been done as outlined in Chapter 8, this should be possible.)
2:00 P.M.	Receive reports from volunteers and staff concerning the completion of tasks assigned in the morning. *IF APPLICABLE SEE TO THE FOLLOWING:*
2:30 P.M.	Rehearse audio/video presentation on site to check for synchronization and timing with the script. Also, check the audio equipment to make sure it is working at a proper volume and without feedback noise. Set up agency's program booth.

Exhibit 9.1 *(continued)*

4:30 P.M.	Staff and volunteers arrive at event site and do the following:
	1. Set up registration area.
	2. Check room setup with catering manager or banquet captain to determine:
	a. Correct number of tables with right number of settings.
	3. If an award event, make sure the actual award is stored at the podium with a copy of the inscription (in large type).
	4. Check setup of reception site—correct number of bars and hors d'oeuvres stations.
	5. Check setup of coat and hat check rooms (especially important on rainy days and during the winter).
	6. Verify that valet parking procedures are established and the drivers know the rules for this event.

Exhibit 9.2 Event Program Time Line

6:30 P.M. ⇓	Reception begins and guests start to check in.
7:20 P.M.	Salads are set on the tables by this time. Lights are blinked and assigned staff and volunteers urge the guests to move into the dining area.
7:30 P.M.	Event chairperson greets guests.
7:34 P.M.	Invocation (if applicable).
7:38 P.M.	VIP greetings (if applicable).
7:42 P.M.	Entrées begin to be served. Dancing begins (this is optional and depends on local custom).
8:46 P.M.	Agency president or designated agency speaker talks about the work of the nonprofit in the community.
8:55 P.M.	Formal program commences. (This next sequence is very important to follow; many guests will leave the dinner after the entrée has been served if the honoree has already received the award. You do not want to lose your audience—it is very embarrassing for everyone.) Keynote speaker (or entertainer) is introduced.
8:57 P.M.	Keynote/entertainer begins.
9:21 P.M.	Honoree is introduced and award is given.
9:26 P.M.	Honoree accepts and responds.
9:32 P.M.	Closing remarks and benediction (if applicable).
9:36 P.M.	Dancing commences.
10:30–11:00 P.M.	Dancing ends (depending on crowd).

Exhibit 9.3   Event Time Line

	National Philanthropy Day Script **Fairmont Hotel—Grand Ballroom** **Friday, November 21, 1997**
	SALADS ARE SET ON TABLES
11:45:	Lights *B*L*I*N*K*E*D* and a trumpet fanfare
Noon:	Another trumpet fanfare
Noon–12:05:	Welcome from Peter M. Drake, Chairman • Thank everyone for their support • Thank honorees and awardees *FIVE-MINUTE SCHMOOZE TIME—* *INTRODUCE YOURSELF TO YOUR NEIGHBOR*
12:10:	Another trumpet fanfare
12:10–12:14:	Drake introduces Tom Boyden, President, Golden Gate Chapter • President, "That Man May See"
12:14–12:17:	Welcoming remarks by Tom Boyden • How NPD benefits the community and profession
12:17:	Tom Boyden remains at podium.
12:17–12:18:	Tom Boyden introduces James C. Hormel, Honorary Chair • 1996's philanthropist of the year • President's nominee as Ambassador to Luxembourg
12:18–12:23:	Remarks by Honorary Chairman James C. Hormel
12:23–12:24:	Drake introduces Terilyn Joe and Dan Ashley, Masters of Ceremonies
12:24–12:39:	Terilyn and Dan read names of honorees and organizations • Medallion given to each honoree Terilyn and Dan tell everyone to enjoy their lunch
12:25:	Entrée served.
12:45–12:47:	Emcees Terilyn and Dan begin award program: • Introduce awardees as follows:
	Emcees ask Charleen Harvey (last year's recipient) to come to the podium to introduce Beatrice Wong: 1997's Outstanding Volunteer Fund Raiser
12:47–12:52	Beatrice C. Wong accepts award of Outstanding Volunteer Fund Raiser
	Emcees Terilyn and Dan ask Jerry Mapp (last year's recipient) to come to the podium to introduce Virginia Carollo Rubin, Director of Development, Exploratorium: 1997's Outstanding Fund Raising Executive
12:53–12:58:	Virginia Carollo Rubin accepts award of Outstanding Fund-Raising Executive
	Terilyn and Dan ask Marilyn Bancel, Chair, Golden Gate Chapter's Awards Committee, to come to the podium.

Exhibit 9.3 *(continued)*

Marilyn Bancel calls to podium, one at a time, the following awardees and presents the award:
12:59–1:04:   Rosenberg Foundation: Outstanding Foundation *Grantmaker. Award accepted and response by: Kirke Wilson, Executive Director*
1:05–1:10:   Charles Schwab & Co.: Outstanding Corporate *Grantmaker. Award accepted and response by: Jim Losi, Senior Vice President, Employee Communications and Community Relations*
1:11–1:16:   Positive Directions Equals Change. The Vineyards Awardee. *Award accepted and response by: Cregg Johnson, Executive Director Terilyn or Dan asks Jim Hormel, Outstanding Philanthropist of 1996, to come to podium to introduce 1997's awardee: Lois M. Dedomenico:*
1:17–1:22:   Outstanding Philanthropist: Lois M. Dedomenico accepts award
1:23–1:27:   Closing remarks by Peter M. Drake

The Event Program Time Line allows for some extra time. If a silent auction is being sponsored, for example, various announcements will be made during the event and winning bidders will have to be recognized.

Events with many honorees and speeches have a different configuration. Exhibit 9.3 depicts just such an event. (I scheduled it for my chapter of the National Society of Fund Raising Executives.) Because many people received awards, the entrée was served during the programming. Exhibit 9.4 is a script that integrates with the Event Time Line; a script can be a separate document or it can be a part of the time line.

METT Checklist for Chapter 9

Week	To Do This Week	Book Ref.	☑
26	Four days before the event, prepare final time line agenda and timed script.		
	Recheck PDQ checklist		

Exhibit 9.4   Chairman's Remarks—Bullet Reminders

	Alan Wendroff's NPD Remarks
12:00–12:03	⇒ Hello, everyone. My name is Alan Wendroff and I have the pleasure of being this year's chair for National Philanthropy Day. Welcome to the Golden Gate Chapter's 10th Anniversary Celebration of this community-wide event. A special thanks for this year's host committee. We would not have gotten off the ground without the assistance of our chapter administrator, Maurine Killough. But I want to give a very warm thank you to a man who started this planning with me as an acquaintance and whom I now consider a friend, the producer of this event: Wayne Strei. One of NSFRE's main purposes is to educate, train, and keep professionals up to date so that they can help donors. We promote philanthropy—our vision is to facilitate the philanthropic process. These professionals generate support for worthy causes that benefit society and especially our community. We also help donors by advising them. At each of your places you will find a copy of "A Donor Bill of Rights"; and by your support of today's luncheon, you also celebrate our donors. And, if you are a donor, we thank you!!
12:04	It is now my pleasure to introduce the president of the golden gate chapter, Glenn Essex. Glenn founded Essex and Drake in 1977. He is a leader in the philanthropic community and has been a professional for 35 years.
12:07	Introduce Claude Rosenberg.
12:13	Introduce Terilyn Joe and Dan Ashley: If you watch Channel Seven News, and who doesn't, you know the next people who will take over this podium, this year's masters of ceremonies: Terilyn Joe and Dan Ashley
1:23	Closing remarks.
Thank you for attending. Goodbye and have a wonderful weekend.	

CONCLUSION

Success is in the details! The combination of the PDQ Checklist and the Event Day Time Line shows what should be accomplished on the event day. Are all of the tips on detail going to make the event foolproof? No. But they will make the event so close to perfect that only the planning staff will know what has gone awry. Such careful planning will allow the planners to make changes for the next event, so they can come close to nirvana.

CHAPTER TEN

Thank You and Goodbye!

INTRODUCTION

This is the evaluation chapter, but there is more to do after the event than just evaluation. The following tasks must be accomplished: (1) acknowledgments; (2) finance; and (3) evaluation.

ALWAYS SAY THANK YOU!

People in many agencies have looked at me skeptically when I suggested that they mail thank-you acknowledgments to all the guests who attended their event, volunteers who helped the agency put it on, event committee members who marketed the event, and co-chairs (thanked by the chair) and the event chair (by the president of the agency). Common courtesy should be the first thought in the minds of the nonprofit's board members when thanking all of the people involved with the event. The second thought should be the golden opportunity an agency has in contacting these people again and leaving them with another good feeling about the nonprofit's work. The best thing about acknowledgments is the ease of accomplishing them; computers make the job easy and doable beforehand. Staff members or volunteers input guests' reservations into the log; at that point it is easy to add guests' addresses so that later the event staff can produce a letter and merge it with the address. Most database programs have some form of mail merge functions that enables users to write form letters.

HOW TO SAY THANK YOU

Now that the agency has decided to thank everyone, what does the letter say? Exhibit 10.1 (⬛CH1001.DOC) is a sample of a generic thank-you/acknowledgment letter.

Let us go through each section so that the fine points of thanking a donor will become clearer.

1. Salutation

    If the guest or volunteer is known to the person(s) signing the letter, use the first or preferred nickname; otherwise, use Dear Mrs./Ms./Mr./Dr. Always try to personalize this letter, but only if the signer knows the guest or volunteer. If there is no connection, it is better to address the letter formally. Many people are secretly picky about how they are addressed by strangers; it is better to err on the side of formality.

Exhibit 10.1   Thank You Letter: An Example

John & Linda Contributor
No. One Philanthropy Place
San Francisco, CA

Dear John and Linda,

Thank you for your generous support of Alpha Charity's tribute to Ben Bigbucks. This is your tenth year of continuous attendance at this event; and on behalf of the board of directors and the staff of Alpha Charity we want you to know how much we appreciate your loyalty.

We know you noticed in the brochure at the table the description of the new homeless program we started this year to help people learn new career skills. This program supplements our ongoing work with the displaced and homeless population in San Francisco.

We heard from Joe and Kathy Prospect who sat at your table. Because of your enthusiastic comments about our agency and your understanding of our work, they made an additional contribution and volunteered to attend and work at next year's dinner.

This year's dinner raised $101,500, a new record! We could not have done it without your help. Again, thanks for your continued support.

Sincerely,

Peter P. Philanthropist   Rosemarie Ready
Chairman, Board of Directors   Executive Director, Alpha Charity

2. Opening paragraph

Thank the addressee immediately—this way it is done, and the letter can proceed to bigger and more important subjects:

Recognize the person's past support to the nonprofit; attendance at the last special event; advertisement in the program journal; or excellent assistance as a volunteer.

3. Second paragraph

State the work of the nonprofit, plus any new programs the agency wants to highlight; in the example, a brochure on a new program is enclosed.

4. Third paragraph

Mention any personal information; in the example, the event followed the classic technique of having a member of its board (local or national) sitting at that table and engaging the guests in conversation about the agency, hence, learning about the attendees interest in volunteering. This paragraph can be written and stored on the computer and inserted when required. If this paragraph is not applicable, then expand the second paragraph with more detail about the agency's programs, ongoing and new.

5. The closing paragraph

   Thank the supporter again and mention the amount of funds raised (especially if it is a record amount).

6. The signature paragraph

   The acknowledgement letter should always be signed by the event chair or the agency president, sometimes both. If the agency executive is active in the nonprofit's programmatic or development areas or is an expert in the agency's particular field, then he or she also should sign the letter. Every agency has its own traditions about how much exposure its executive should receive; those unwritten rules will govern if he or she signs letters like this.

Some agencies do not have the staff or volunteers to personalize acknowledgment letters. But they still want and need to thank their supporters. What to do? Postcards will do the job. While they are not the best way, at least the paying guests and volunteers will receive a message from the nonprofit, which is better than no message at all. If postcards are chosen, make them different and somewhat original, like the one seen in Exhibit 10.2.

Another way to make the postcard different is to use a cartoon to get the message across. Designer postcards look much better than generic ones. They can be printed more cheaply than running them through the agency's computer printer. To be unique, send an e-mail thank you through one of the many greeting card Web sites: go to a search engine and use these words: Thank you and greeting.

Very often after testimonial dinners, the honoree wants to send a thank-you letter to all the attendees. This letter is an additional thank you and gives the nonprofit another opportunity to communicate with its supporters. It is a welcome addition to the communication stream, and an honoree should be encouraged to send this letter (if possible, on his or her own letterhead.) Exhibit 10.3 (🔒CH1003.DOC) is an exam-

---

Exhibit 10.2   Thank You Postcard

AGENCY LOGO AND ADDRESS/TELEPHONE, FAX & E-MAIL NO./ADDRESS

We were having so much fun
at the dinner & auction
we might not have
thanked you.
THANKS!

Peter P. Philanthropist   Rosemarie Ready

---

ple of this type of letter. The honoree is expressing once again (he acknowledged the honor at the event) his warm feelings for the agency and emphasizing the importance of the award. By sending this letter, the honoree is telling the community, from an objective point of view, how much the work of the nonprofit is accomplishing.

FINANCE

There is nothing more aggravating to the event leadership or the professional staff than to have to wait a week or more for the event's final financial report. If the reservation log has been kept up to date and the revenue has been tallied on a weekly basis, there is really no excuse for delays.

The next working day after the event should be the time when the invoices are mailed to the outstanding accounts; these invoices can be generated through the computer program just as the thank-you letters are printed. The expense items should all be added up from the submitted invoices; the major invoice usually will be the one from the caterer or hotel. An informal handwritten copy is almost always given to the agency on the day of the event, since it needs a signature in order for a formal invoice to be prepared and mailed. By the event day, all other expense invoices will have been submitted.

Now that the agency knows all sources of income—income received and income invoiced, plus the total expenses—it is a no-brainer to prepare an income statement using the revenue and expense budget form (Exhibit 3.1). In fact, it is possible to link the reservation log with a blank revenue and expense budget form at the beginning of the reservation process so that all revenue is recorded as it is received. Expenses also can be inputted either through the reservation log or through a special expense log.

Important Tip

All checks and cash must be deposited the day they are received. Most agencies have established procedures for this type of accounting, but for those who have not, please do so ASAP! It will save a lot of headaches for all concerned. Deposits are another way to verify the total income. If an agency has only one bank account, try to make the special event deposits separate from the general agency ones.

EVALUATION

Evaluation, or determining the worth of a special event, can be a valuable exercise if all the people involved participate in the process. They must make candid observations, be willing to follow through and help

Exhibit 10.3   Thank You Letter From Honoree: An Example
_____

ONE MARKET
R E S T A U R A N T

June 20, 1994

Mr. & Mrs. Alan Wendroff
1028 De Haro Street
San Francisco, CA 94107

Dear Alan and Lyllian:

Receiving the Anti-Defamation League's Restaurant Industry Achievement Award
on June 6 was truly more than I could have dreamed of 15 years ago when I made
my first professional foray into the restaurant world. The honor is especially
meaningful, though, because of your support of my receiving the award and your
attendance, with me, at the awards dinner.

With your help, the event raised nearly $50,000 to aid ADL's fight against bigotry
and discrimination.

Thank you, Alan and Lyllian, for all your support.

Warmly,

Michael

1 MARKET STREET, SAN FRANCISCO, CALIFORNIA 94105-1572
RESTAURANT (415) 777-5577 • OFFICE 777-5588 • FAX 777-4411
_____

Used with permission from One Market Restaurant, San Francisco.

correct the mistakes and deficiencies, and assist in making the next event a better fund-raising program. If the special event came close to, met, or exceeded its monetary goals, then the evaluation can act as a motivation factor for everyone concerned, lay leaders and professional staff. If the event was just a run-of-the-mill affair—for example, if just a bare-bones profit was raised or participants just seemed to be going through the motions—then someone, such as the nonprofit's president or executive director or the event chair, is going to have to provide strong leadership and motivation to move the process along. The agency will want to overcome the lethargy that has set in and make the next event a successful, upbeat affair.

The executive committee evaluating the event should schedule a meeting no later than one week after the event, so that everything that took place is fresh in people's minds. It is good objective practice to poll a cross section of the people who volunteered in putting the event on and guests and members of the professional staff (with the iron-clad guarantee that their answers will be anonymous). This poll should deal with organization, style, ambiance, and content of the event. The monetary results are objective and easy to evaluate when compared to the planned goals.

Some of the questions that should be asked of volunteers:

- Were they given adequate training in the tasks they were asked to do? Did a volunteer coordinator manage their assignments? Was this person available to answer questions and solve problems promptly?
- What did he or she think of the ambiance—the room decor, table setup, and quality of food and service?
- What did he or she think of the content of the event program?

Ask guests:

- How were they received at the event? (This question is especially important for those who attended alone.) Many guests may not have known the other guests, and it is imperative that they were made to feel at home.
- How was the food and service?
- Why did they attend the event?

This survey can be started almost immediately by having a senior staff member ask some guests, informally, during a conversation at the table or while leaving the event, or by telephone one or two afterward. This input is valuable because it is usually very objective; no matter how hard members of the executive committee who are conducting an evaluation try to be objective, since they were responsible for the event—it was their baby—they cannot help being subjective. Committee members should combine all the answers in creating Exhibit 10.4, Evaluation Goals (CH1004.DOC).

A Special Note on Evaluating Expenses

The evaluation of special event expenses is an exercise that should be ongoing from the day the event budget is written. The "Calculating Expenses" section in Chapter 3 explains the methodology to use in obtaining a realistic expense figure for a particular item. If the research is done and a cost per item is obtained—the lowest quote for the same quality, delivered on the desired date—then the only way to lower the cost is to obtain the item as an in-kind gift. If a particular item costs more than what was planned, then the agency has made an error. For example, the agency may deliver the copy and final advertisement graphics to the printer later than agreed upon. In order to get the material to the event on time, the agency will incur express delivery charges that bring the cost over the original estimate. This situation has to be factored in for the next event. Except for this type of cost overrun, expenses should not be a part of the postevent evaluation; rather, expenses should be evaluated daily or weekly.

The evaluation committee's most important job is to interpret the answers and write a report to the board and development committee so that any problems can be addressed before the next event. The actual results shown in Exhibit 10.4 are not from an actual event, but examples to show how to evaluate the particular item. In order for this type of evaluation to be meaningful, the evaluators have to be critical within the parameters of what they instructed the vendors or volunteers to do. If an agency *thought* it was to receive certain extras from the caterer but did not specifically write them into the contract or send a memo to the catering manager, then when the extra is not forthcoming they cannot mark down the evaluation.

TIP: Take nothing for granted!!

Evaluating the Evaluation

The factual answers and the subjective observations derived from Exhibit 10.4 allow the agency to target problems that arose during the event and take advantage of the pluses that resulted from the good

Exhibit 10.4   Evaluation Goals: Form

Category/ Evaluation Subject	Planned Result	Actual Result	% of Planned Result
GOALS:			
AMOUNT OF MONEY RAISED:			
Individual reservations	$67,500	$65,750	97
Premium Tables (total gold & silver)	$15,000	$20,000	133
Donations	$3,000	$3,600	120
Advertisements (Ad Journal)	$10,000	$11,500	115
In-Kind Gifts	$5,000	$4,500	90
TOTAL	$100,500	$105,350	105
VOLUNTEER PERFORMANCE:	OBJECTIVE	RESULT	
Training	Adequate to perform the task	Excellent	
Management	On-the-spot problem solver	Good	
Were there enough volunteers to complete the job?		Good	
CATERING AND ROOM AMBIANCE:	OBJECTIVE	RESULT	
Quality of servings	Fresh and tasty	Excellent	
Presentation on table	Neat and uncluttered	Very good	
Waiter service	Quick, accurate, and unobtrusive	Excellent	
Room decor & setup	As planned with catering manager	Standard	
PROGRAM NOTES:			
Did the event start and finish on time?	Enough time was allocated for each speaker & audio/video presentation	Very good	
Was the sound system adequate?	Was everyone able to hear the speakers; no microphone feedback	Substandard	

Exhibit 10.4 *(continued)*

Category/ *Evaluation Subject*	*Planned Result*	*Actual Result*	*% of Planned Result*
MISCELLANEOUS:			
Coat and hat check:	Were there enough people on duty?	Excellent	
Valet parking	Promptness and courtesy	Very good	
Reception area	Everyone was given their assigned seat; no hassles with last-minute guests	Excellent	

strategy that was followed during the weeks leading up to it. One of the most important goals was raising funds, and the exhibit outlines the results of the organization efforts that led to the total revenue. The following observations can be made based on the revenue lines:

1. Individual reservations were 3 percent under the planned goal. Why? When revenue is less than the anticipated goal by a small percentage, it usually indicates that the event committee members failed to follow-through and make telephone calls (METT Week 22) in the last two or three weeks before event day. It also indicates reservations were not checked against the names provided by committee members in the last two or three weeks prior to event day. Perhaps the rush of reservations during this period overwhelmed the agency's support staff; perhaps some committee members just refused to follow-through. Usually, 10 to 25 percent of the committee members provide only their own reservations; unless they are motivated by a telephone call from one of the senior event chairs, they may no longer focus on the event. Keeping the senior event co-chairs targeted on committee member follow-up can make up small percentages, such as the 3 percent in the example. If reservations fall off more than 5 percent, then something is happening that requires follow-up with the event committee chair and members. If this is a testimonial event, the problem might be that the honoree was not as well known in the community as suggested in the initial planning

meeting. Evaluators also must look at scheduling; holding an event in the middle of the local "high" fund-raising season can produce unique problems, especially if sister organizations are having an event that has a mainstream entertainer or speaker. Look at the agency's marketing efforts and measure them against the marketing plan outlined in Chapter 6. Also, check whether the event was overpriced. If event admission price is $250 per seat and other local organizations are charging $150— well, the answer is clear, the event outpriced itself.

2. In-kind gifts are the other revenue source that fell behind the planned result, and by an amount that is hard to overlook: 10 percent. Was a list of items needed for the event made, and were names of more than two possible vendors found for each item? Check on the number of prospective vendors that the co-chair was planning to contact versus the number actually contacted. In cases where contacts were made and vendors decided not to participate in the event, check whether someone who had a peer relationship with the vendor's executive made contact. Due to lower revenue in the in-kind gift line, expenses increased, and thus the net income the event produced for the agency was lowered.

Had individual reservations met the planned goal and had in-kind gifts been in the amount expected, the event would have raised a total of $107,600, a healthy 7 percent above planned revenue. This extra amount could come in very handy if there was an unforeseen increase in an expense item.

Evaluating Volunteers

The next goal for evaluation is volunteer performance. This is a very delicate area. Board members and professional staff recruit volunteers because of the latters' interest in helping the agency. Sometimes these volunteers are major agency supporters and sit on the board of directors. Why do they volunteer to help at the special event? For two reasons: They want to see firsthand whether the event, which is taking the professional's time away from other duties, is worthwhile and successful, and they want to determine if a special event does produce the seven goals they were told it would achieve.

Ideal volunteers arrive at the special event when scheduled, listen to instructions, and perform their duty as required. If they have questions, they ask someone before they act. Here the agency must provide leadership; agencies that plan to rely on volunteers to perform vital jobs at an event must have a volunteer coordinator. The three items—training, management, and number of volunteers—that are evaluated here relate to that leadership goal: A happy volunteer is one who knows where to go, what to do, and how to do it.

Tip

If too many volunteers turn up, release some from their scheduled duties and let them enjoy themselves at the event. Do not let volunteers stand around doing nothing; they will feel misused and out of place, and most important, they will never volunteer again!

Evaluating Ambiance

Next the catering and room ambiance is evaluated. In other words, did the food taste good and was the room pleasant to be in, and oh yes, did the waitpersons do a good job?

Did the food taste good? By whose and what standards is this to be judged? Everyone's taste buds are different (except for chocolate in any form). What to do? Here we have to rely on the basics. For example, all salads must be served fresh—the greens must be crisp. Second, the entrées must be served at the correct temperature for the particular item and placed on the plate in a pleasing manner—no plate should look like it came directly from an army mess hall. This is why the specifications to the caterer for every event should include a preview meal.

The appearance of the table itself is equally important, as it is the first thing guests see when they sit down for the meal. Before the design is checked, make sure that there is the correct amount of silverware, plates, and condiment containers. Then, when the adequate elements are on the table, how does it look? The next item to look at is the table decoration. One of the seven goals is to promote the agency to the community; if the guests can talk to each other, this goal can be achieved. But if the table decorations block sight lines and make conversation possible only with the person on each side of the guest, then one of the purposes of producing a special event is defeated.

Waitperson service should be quick, accurate, and unobtrusive. The ultimate in quick service means that every table is served at the same time. Doing this is virtually impossible and economically wasteful, unless a waitperson is allocated for each table. Waitpersons usually are responsible for four tables; they can serve all four tables swiftly if they have busperson backup. This is the evaluation criteria for waitpersons.

Room decor and design—the wall spaces and floral decorations used to lighten up the room and as room dividers—are evaluated according to the plan set up with the catering manager. This will be no problem if the outline in Chapter 7 is followed. After the catering staff has set up the room, check the number of tables and settings at each one. Check that the correct room dividers have been used and that all the bars and hors d'oeuvres stations have been set up.

Evaluating the Program

Timing is crucial when producing a special event. Was the time allocated to the speakers and audio/video presentations adequate for the purpose? Was the agenda followed—did the event start and end on time?

Sound systems are sometimes the source of great annoyance with high-pitched squeals and microphone feedback. Did the technician know how to modulate the equipment to achieve the correct volume so that everyone could hear what was going on? If the room is large, a trial run is in order.

Evaluating the Miscellaneous Items

Miscellaneous items provide creature comfort to the guests. Often they are overlooked during evaluations, but upon reflection, the entire ambiance of the event depends on each segment being excellent. Coat and hat check, valet parking, and of course the work of the reception staff of volunteers and professionals are vital for a successful event.

METT Checklist for Chapter 10

Week	To Do This Week	Book Ref.	☑
27	Thank you to all concerned.		
	Evaluation of event.		

CONCLUSION

If conducted within one week after an event, evaluations can be invaluable in planning the next event. All agencies that produce special events should have a file folder for event logistics in their computer word processing program and a copy in a binder for everyone to refer to in future months and years. Special events can provide an agency with the needed money and volunteers to plan a solid future and growth that will be so necessary for nonprofit agencies in the twenty-first century.

Special Resources

SPECIAL EVENT RESOURCES

The resources listed in this section will assist your agency and help it produce the special events that will give your organization the success in all of the objectives that are outlined in the Seven Goals in the Introduction.
We will cover four areas:

- Documents that will guide your organization
- Computer software information that can be put to use almost immediately
- Organizations to contact for information about fund raising and nonprofit management
- A bibliography of texts that the author considers to be the most helpful to an agency in developing their fund raising plans.

DOCUMENTS

The Master Event Timetable (METT) is the navigator for all the events described in this book. When an event is first conceived, and the preliminary strategy is developed, it must be fit into a structure of time, and then scheduled to completion of the special event. The details on how the METT can help do this are described in Chapter 1, both theoretically and then applied to an actual event, Dinner à la Heart. At the end of each chapter there is a METT checklist indicating tasks to do during the week(s) that apply to the chapter's subject.

How to write and Evaluate a Fund Raising Letter gives the development director a structure and some pointers on how to write and format a fund raising letter, and just about all other types of letters related to fund raising, and especially special events.

The Mission Statement from the Goldman Institute on Aging is an excellent example of succinctness, statement of values, and clarity of purpose. I cannot emphasize too much the importance to your nonprofit of a well written mission statement, one that clarifies the nonprofit's values and commitments to the community.

The sample press release gives you an idea of what type of subject can be written about (and how to write about it) in order to "plug" the special event. Linking the special event with an underwriter or a sponsor is smart marketing. The nonprofit achieves a goal from the support of the underwriter or sponsor and in turn the association of the underwriter or sponsor with the nonprofit is an added bonus for them. Look at it as another way to say, "thank you."

COMPUTER SOFTWARE

There is nothing more frustrating than purchasing a software program and then finding out that it is so complex that your staff cannot use it to its full advantage. There are many software programs designed for the fund raising (development) office of a nonprofit. Most of these programs will keep track of your contributors, past, present, and future prospects. They will also provide special modules for accounting and special events, etc., only if the agency owns the full software package. But, if your nonprofit already has a system up and running that provides the organization with contributor information and the agency only requires a program for special events, there was very little to choose from, until the Spring of 1998 when Certain Software published Event Planner Plus™, a window based application. The author was an *unpaid* reviewer, alpha and beta tester for this program, and can assure the reader that there are many features found in this program that will help the nonprofit produce a successful special event: Event Planner Plus' Event Wizard for setting up your event, a budget control that compares revenue to expense and what expenses are outstanding, plus over 25 printable management reports; the program is reasonably priced.

Certain Software
One Daniel Burnham Court, Suite 330C
San Francisco, CA 94109-5460
Tel: (415) 353-5330
Fax: (415) 353-5355
E-Mail: *tarbuckle@certain.com*
www.certain.com

Many nonprofit agencies do not have the extra funds to purchase a special program for special events. They do, however, have computer capabilities, which is why this book provides a model special event log and other reports, that can be produced with your own spreadsheet or database program. These reports are not fancy, but they will produce management information that will allow your agency to keep track of its special event.

There are other software programs designed for unique special events, like auctions, and golf tournaments, etc. The author has not tried these programs, so I cannot comment on them. However, if one looks like it will work for your agency, ask the publisher to send a trial demonstration copy, before investing your money.

Professional Organizations
for Nonprofit Agencies

American Association of Fund-Raising Counsel
25 West 43rd Street, Suite 820
New York, NY 10036
Tel: (212) 354-5799

AAFRC publishes the annual report *Giving USA* that measures the
   state of American Philanthropy
Association for Health Care Philanthropy
313 Park Avenue, Suite 400
Falls Church, VA 22046
Tel: (703) 532-6243

Independent Sector
1828 I Street, N.W.
Washington, D.C. 20036
Tel: (202) 223-8100
Web site: www.indepsec.org

National Society of Fund Raising Executives (NSFRE)
1101 King Street, Suite 700
Alexandria, VA 22314-2967
Tel: (703) 684-0410
Web site: www.nsfre.org

NSFRE Advances Philanthropy through Education, Training, and
   Advocacy; certifies professional fund raisers (CFRE) and is the
   largest professional fund raising association in the United States.
   Check the Web site for the location of your local chapter.
National Center for Nonprofit Boards
2000 'L' Street, Suite 510
Washington, D.C. 20036-4907
Web site: www.ncnb.org

The Foundation Center
79 Fifth Avenue
New York, NY 10003-3076
Web site: www.fdncenter.org
The Foundation Center is a national service organization that provides
   a source of information on foundations and corporate giving. The
   Center maintains library's around the country; telephone: 1-800-
   424-9836 for the collection nearest your community.

For nonprofits who are Internet savvy and communicate with volunteers and supporters by e-mail on a regular basis, the following sites
can be very valuable:

To send a greeting or thank you: www.greetingsonline.com
For animated greeting cards for various occasions: www. bluemountain.com
To send flowers—real or via e-mail—go to Norton's Flowers Web site: www.emailflowers.com

Nonprofit Newspapers

The Chronicle of Philanthropy
Web site: www.philanthropy.com
An indispensable publication for nonprofit professionals.
NonProfit Times
Web site: nptimes.com

REFERENCE BIBLIOGRAPHY

Drucker, Peter F., *Managing the Nonprofit Organization—Principles and Practice.* (New York: HarperCollins, 1990).

Freedman, Harry A. and Feldman, Karen, *The Business of Special Events: Fundraising Strategies for Changing Times.* (Sarasota, Florida: Pineapple Press, Inc., 1998).

If you are putting on celebrity special events, this book should be in your library.
Grace, Kay Sprinkel, *Beyond Fund Raising—New Strategies for Nonprofit Innovation and Investment.* (New York: John Wiley & Sons, Inc., 1997).

This book will give you and your organization the best insight into stewardship practices that really work.
Landskroner, Ronald A., *The Nonprofit Manager's Resource Directory.* (New York: John Wiley & Sons, Inc., 1996).

Levy, Barbara R., et al. (eds.), *The NSFRE Fund-Raising Dictionary.* (New York: John Wiley & Sons, Inc., 1996).

Mixer, Joseph R., *Principles of Professional Fundraising—Useful Foundations for Successful Practice.* (San Francisco, CA: Jossey-Bass, Inc., 1993).

Rosenberg Jr., Claude, *Wealthy and Wise: How you and America can get the most out of your giving.* (New York: Little, Brown & Company, 1994).

Once the major givers have attended your special event, then learn how to talk to them in language they can understand.
Rosso, Henry A., and Associates, *Achieving Excellence in Fund Raising.* (San Francisco, CA: Jossey-Bass, Inc., 1991).

This is fund raising 101 plus! A must read for all fledgling fund raisers and a great reference for the rest of us.

Stern, Gary J., *Marketing Workbook for Nonprofit Organizations.* (St. Paul, MN: Amherst H. Wilder Foundation, 1990).

An excellent workbook for basic information and techniques on nonprofit marketing.

Zinsser, William K., *On Writing Well.* (New York: HarperCollins, 1994, Fifth Edition).

On Writing Well has nothing specific to do with Special Events. But, it is an indispensable guide for every person who wants to express themselves in writing with clear, concise, understandable sentences and paragraphs, without clutter but with style.

A Weekly Schedule of Tasks to Achieve a *Successful* Special Event

Week	To Do This Week	Responsible	☑
One	a) Governing board sets up Special Event Committee		
	b) Select Type of Special Event for your agency		
	c) Event Chairperson is recruited		
	d) Complete revenue & expense budget		
	e) Recruit Honoree and/or Special Guest(s)		
	f) Prepare Event Timetable		
	g) Update agency's Mission Statement (if needed)		
	Set date & choose site for your event		
Two	a) Chairperson recruits co-chairs		
	b) Prepare preliminary list of prospective names for event committee and invitation list		
	c) Set up computer program		
Three	a) Recruit Honorary co-chairs		
	b) Complete co-chair recruitment		
	c) Set date for Event Chair & Co-Chair meeting		
	d) Obtain additional names from Chair & Co-Chairs		
Four	a) Establish marketing & public relations guidelines		
	b) Prepare press releases		
	c) Prepare Save the Date notices		
	d) Prepare draft of event invitation package		
Five	a) Agenda for event Chair & Co-Chairs meeting		
	b) Chair & Co-Chair to provide additional names for Event Committee		
	c) Set date for "one and only" Event Committee meeting		
	d) Discuss Other Sources of Revenue with Event Chair and co-Chairs		
Six	a) Start negotiations with site and catering managers		
	b) Continue recruiting committee members		
	c) Obtain insurance and governmental permits		
	d) Mail "Save the Date" notice to all names		

A Weekly Schedule of Tasks to Achieve a *Successful* Special Event *(continued)*

Week	To Do This Week	Responsible	☑
Seven	a) Select printer and mailing house		
	b) Determine size & layout of invitation package		
	c) Determine how many volunteers are required and outline their duties		
	d) Continue recruiting committee members through week 9		
	e) Work with ad journal co-chair and set up solicitation campaign		
Eight	a) Prepare event committee information kits		
Nine	a) Mail Event Committee invitation letters		
Ten	a) Continue to add names to event invitation list through week 16		
Eleven⇓	a) Start monoriting reservations from Dinner Committee mailing re: Budget		
Twelve⇓	⇓		
Thirteen⇓	⇓		
Fourteen⇓	a) Event Committee meeting (one and only meeting)		
Fifteen⇓	a) Telephone and/or Fax committee members and ask them to send their mailing lists to you ASAP!!		
Sixteen	a) Arrange site layout, sound & decorating		
Seventeen	a) Complete in-kind solicitations		
Eighteen	a) Event invitations mailed		
	b) Follow up with event committee members and other prospects		
Nineteen	a) Event committee members mail personal letters to prospects		
Twenty	a) Prepare check list for items & people you need at event		
Twenty-one	a) First deadline for ad journal copy; telephone all advertisers that have not submitted camera ready ad		
Twenty-two	a) Start FINAL PUSH telephone campaign for reservations and event journal ads		
Twenty-three	a) Final deadline for ad copy and camera ready material		

A Weekly Schedule of Tasks to Achieve a *Successful* Special Event *(continued)*

Week	To Do This Week		Responsible	☑
Twenty-four	a)	Reconfirm all speaker and special guests arrangements		
Twenty-five	a)	Bring everything altogether—You are almost there!		
Twenty-six	a)	"EVENT DAY"		
Twenty-seven	a)	Acknowledgments—Thank everyone involved!		

HOW TO WRITE AND EVALUATE A FUND RAISING LETTER

Personalize: If addressee is known by the signer, personalize the salutation with their usual name (or nickname); at the next level, use Ms., Mrs., or Mr. Try to remark on the addressee's relationship with the nonprofit, i.e., *"Thank you for your past support; your in-kind gift for the auction,"* etc. Signer should be an officer of the board, a board member, or a current supporter. Professional staff (except prominent "celebrity" staff, e.g., the Maestro of the Symphony) should never sign a fund raising letter.

Objectivity: Whether you are asking for a specific amount, an unspecified gift, or an offer to purchase a ticket, state the specific object of the letter in the beginning, middle, and ending paragraphs.

Be Succinct: Keep letter to one page. This usually works best with fund raising letters. If you have a suggested gift schedule, print it on a return card or envelope and insert it with the letter

Clarity: Write short paragraphs and sentences. Use normal, everyday words that bring clarity to the object of your letter.

Variety: Use a variety of normal words. Make the construction of the paragraph and sentence interesting by using <u>underlines,</u> dashes – and a clear typeface, like Arial Narrow in 11 point type. If the letter is exceptionably short, use 12 or 14 point type; exclamation marks; different layout of words or integrated with a symbol and varied by using bold and normal highlighting: AlanL.**WENDROFF**CFRE☐Consultant.

Stress: Make important points stand out by your choice of words. Stress those words by making them BOLD AND *ITALICIZED.*

Urgency: If the letter offers something like tickets to a theater party or a performance, insert a sense of urgency by indicating a *cutoff date* or limited time to respond to the offer.

Comprehension: When the addressees finish reading the letter they should know exactly what is expected of them; what action they should take and how to do it.

Postscript: If possible, always use a *handwritten* postscript! But, a postscript is vital so use one even if it is typed. Surveys indicate that the majority of your audience will read the P.S. before they read the body of the letter.

Envelope: If possible *hand address* the envelope; the next best method is a typed addressed envelope—never use a label. Use a stamp! The post office has a large variety of beautiful stamps. If at all possible, avoid a printed, mechanical stamp.

GOLDMAN INSTITUTE ON AGING
Mount Zion Health Systems, Inc.

Mission Statement

"Helping Seniors Live Independently"

The mission of the Goldman Institute On Aging is to assure that people, as they age, be as healthy and independent as possible. To realize this mission, we create and provide innovative programs in health, social services, education, and research. These programs enable older adults to remain in their homes and communities while living life fully.

In furthering our mission, we develop partnerships with the community in order to help us achieve a society that promotes the dignity of older adults and supports their caregivers.

Values

In fulfilling this mission, we make the following commitments:

To the people we serve: We promise you our respect, caring and concern in all of our interactions. We will treat you with dignity, honor your individual life choices and endeavor to bring joy and humor into your lives. Our commitment is to continually expand our knowledge and skills so that we can offer you the highest quality professional services.

To the communities in which we live and work: We promise to advocate for needed services and programs and strive to create strong collaborative relationships with other community organizations. We will maintain financial stability and actively raise funds to ensure our continued services and reliability.

To each other: We recognize the importance of each of our contributions, with appreciation and support. We will communicate openly and directly and generously share information. We will seek, cherish and nurture diversity in our backgrounds and experiences which enhances the responsiveness of our services.

To those who support us: We recognize that your time, money and concern for older adults make our work possible, and we endeavor to utilize these resources wisely. Working together, we can make a difference in the lives of the older adults in our communities.

These values and commitments guide our decisions and behaviors.

Master Event Timetable: Blank

Week	To Do This Week	Responsible	☑
One			
Two			
Three			
Four			
Five			
Six			
Seven			

Master Event Timetable *(continued)*

Week	*To Do This Week*	*Responsible*	☑
Eight			
Nine			
Ten			
Eleven			
Twelve			
Thirteen			
Fourteen			
Fifteen			
Sixteen			
Seventeen			
Eighteen			
Nineteen			
Twenty			
Twenty-one			
Twenty-two			
Twenty-three			
Twenty-four			
Twenty-five			
Twenty-six			
Twenty-seven			

ALPHA CHARITY
Anywhere U.S.A.

URGENT FOR IMMEDIATE RELEASE
LOCAL CORPORATION (LOCORP) FUNDS ALPHA'S ANNUAL DINNER DANCE
For details contact: Pete Relations—415-123-4567

SAN FRANCISCO, CA—October 7, 1998. The Alpha Charity's 10th annual dinner dance and silent auction will be held on Thursday, December 31, 1998. This traditional alcoholic free New Years Eve event supports addiction free clinics throughout the San Francisco Bay Area. Known as the safe way to celebrate New Years Eve, the event is supported by every local and state political, community, and corporate leader in the Bay Area. The agency received a boost today when it was announced that Local Corporation (LOCORP) will underwrite the entire catering costs for the annual dinner dance.

Alpha Charity maintains ten addiction free clinics in the following locations: San Francisco, Oakland, Richmond, Walnut Creek, Fremont, Hayward, San Mateo, San Jose, Palo Alto, and San Rafael. Each clinic has a resident, licensed social worker, trained to help alcoholics, drug users, and nicotine addicts kick their habit.

Alpha's mission is to free addicts from their addictions and return these people to their families and professions and the self-realization of good old-fashioned work where they can become economic providers and not takers. For the past ten years, Alpha has relied on private and corporate donations to fund their work. This freedom from public sector funding has allowed Alpha to challenge government programs, and in their quest for an addiction free America, steer the addicts to the path of self-reliance so their dignity can be restored.

LOCORP expects to be joined by other corporations, businesses, and individuals who have traditionally funded the work or who have contributed to the silent auction at Alpha annual dinner dance.

The dinner dance will be held in the grand ballroom of the Bigevent Hotel, located on Russian Hill overlooking the bay. The reception and silent auction begins at 6:30 p.m., dinner and dancing will start at 7:30 p.m. Dress is in the spirit of New Year's Eve: From casual to black tie. For reservations, please call Ben Goodheart, chairman, or Pete Relations at: 415-123-4567

#   #   #

Index

About the Disk

INTRODUCTION

The forms on the enclosed disk are saved in Microsoft Excel version 97, and Microsoft Word for Windows version 7.0. In order to use the forms, you will need to have spreadsheet software capable of reading Microsoft Excel version 97 files, and word processing software capable of reading Microsoft Word for Windows version 7.0 files.

EXHIBITS THAT APPEAR ON THE DISK:

In addition, the following forms will be on the disk from the Resource Section:

SYSTEM REQUIREMENTS

- IBM PC or compatible computer
- 3.5" floppy disk drive
- Windows 95 or later

  Microsoft Excel version 97 or later or other spreadsheet software capable of reading Microsoft Excel 7.0 files.

  NOTE: Files are formatted in Microsoft Excel version 97. To use the worksheets with other spreadsheet programs, refer to the user manual that accompanies your software package for instructions on reading Microsoft Excel files.

• Microsoft Word for Windows version 7.0 or later or other word processing software capable of reading Microsoft Word for Windows 7.0 files.

NOTE: Many popular word processing programs are capable of reading Microsoft Word for Windows 7.0 files. However, users should be aware that a slight amount of formatting might be lost when using a program other than Microsoft Word. If your word processor cannot read Microsoft Word for Windows 7.0 files, unformatted text files have been provided in the TXT directory on the floppy disk.

HOW TO INSTALL THE FILES ONTO YOUR COMPUTER

To install the files follow the instructions below.
1. Insert the enclosed disk into the floppy disk drive of your computer.
2. From the Start Menu, choose **Run.**
3. Type **A:\SETUP** and press **OK.**
4. The opening screen of the installation program will appear. Press **OK** to continue.
5. The default destination directory is C:\SPECIAL. If you wish to change the default destination, you may do so now.
6. Press **OK** to continue. The installation program will copy all files to your hard drive in the C:\SPECIAL or user-designated directory.

USING THE FILES

Loading Files

To use the spreadsheet files, launch your spreadsheet program. Select **File, Open** from the pull-down menu. Select the appropriate drive and directory. If you installed the files to the default directory, the files will be located in the C:\SPECIAL directory. A list of files should appear. If you do not see a list of files in the directory, you need to select **Microsoft Excel Files (*.XLS)** under **Files of Type.** Double click on the file you want to open. Use and edit the file according to your needs.

To use the word processing files, launch your word processing program. Follow the steps above. If you do not see a list of files in the directory, you need to select **WORD DOCUMENT (*.DOC)** under **Files of Type.** Double click on the file you want to open. Edit the file according to your needs.

Printing Files

If you want to print the files, select **File, Print** from the pull-down menu.

Saving Files

When you have finished editing a file, you should save it under a new file name by selecting **File, Save As** from the pull-down menu.

USER ASSISTANCE

If you need assistance with installation or if you have a damaged disk, please contact Wiley Technical Support at:

Phone: (212) 850-6753
Fax: (212) 850-6800 (Attention: Wiley Technical Support)
Email: techhelp@wiley.com

To place additional orders or to request information about other Wiley products, please call (800) 225-5945.

For information about the disk see the **About the Disk** section on page 211.